# NO TIME FOR FIG-LEAVES

## A Comedy

by

DUNCAN GREENWOOD

&

ROBERT KING

SAMUEL  FRENCH

LONDON

NEW YORK TORONTO SYDNEY HOLLYWOOD

ISBN 0 573 01523 6

# NO TIME FOR FIG-LEAVES

First produced by James Cooper of the Renegades Theatre Club, at the Little Theatre, Ilford, on 6th August 1964. Produced by Haymarket Stage Productions Ltd at the Palace Theatre, Westcliff-on-Sea, on 30th August 1965 with the following cast of characters:

(*in the order of their appearance*)

| | |
|---|---|
| MONICA SHARPE, Constance's private secretary | *Peggy Aitchison* |
| CONSTANCE CLAYTHORNE, the Prime Minister | *Barbara Miller* |
| DORA, the servant | *Susanna Pinney* |
| LYDIA PARKER, M.P., Minister of Science | *Pauline Garner* |
| WING COMMANDER NIGEL LAWLER, R.A.F. | *Angus Lennie* |
| MAJOR DANVERS-BISHOP, W.R.A.C. | *Beatrice Shaw* |
| PROFESSOR DAVID MOXTON | *Ken Ward* |
| HELEN MARCHBANKS, W.R.N.S., the First Lord of the Admiralty | *Daphne Odin-Pearse* |
| CORPORAL EVE FORSTER, W.R.A.C. | *Penelope Harris* |

Directed by ALEXANDER BRIDGE

## SYNOPSIS OF SCENES

*The action of the Play passes in the reception-room of Constance Claythorne's country house*

ACT I

A morning in spring

ACT II

Later that day

ACT III

The following afternoon

*Time—the near but unspecified future*

*No Time for Fig-Leaves* — *Set Design by James Cooper* — *Photograph by Bud Parmenter*

# ACT I

SCENE—*The reception-room of Constance Claythorne's country house. A morning in spring in the near but unspecified future.*

*It is a spacious, well-furnished room, tastefully decorated, with french windows back* C *giving access to a terrace with a view of parkland beyond. A door up* L *gives access to the hall and there is another door up* R. *Tall, built-in bookshelves flank the french windows. A sofa stands* RC *with an easy chair to match* R. *There are occasional tables* R, *up* R, *up* L *and* C, *and there is a sideboard with drinks* L. *At night the room is lit by a standard lamp up* R *and a table-lamp* R.

*When the* CURTAIN *rises, it is a bright spring morning and the birds are heard singing through the open french windows.* MONICA SHARPE *is standing at the french windows looking out into the garden. She is in her early thirties, is clever and efficient, but without feminine charm. She is severely dressed in tweeds and has a brief-case under her arm.* CONSTANCE CLAYTHORNE *enters by the french windows. She is a large, impressive-looking woman in late middle-age. She wears a riding habit and carries a riding crop and gloves. She sweeps across to the table* R *and puts down the crop and gloves.*

CONSTANCE. You're lucky to catch me. Dora headed me off at the bottom of the paddock. If I'd gone by the round copse you wouldn't have seen me till lunch-time. I assume it was you who sent her to intercept me?

MONICA. Guilty, I'm afraid. (*She moves to the table* C)

CONSTANCE. Well, I hope it's sufficiently urgent to justify the sacrifice of an hour's ride.

MONICA. I think you'll find it is.

CONSTANCE. If it isn't I shall be looking for a new private secretary.

MONICA (*offended*) That's entirely up to you.

CONSTANCE (*moving below the sofa*) Oh, Monica! Don't take me so damned literally. If you disrupt my week-end you must expect me to be irritable.

MONICA (*picking up some papers from the table* C) It can wait till after lunch if that's more convenient. (*She is about to put the papers in her brief-case*)

CONSTANCE. It isn't. I'm rowing from two till three, swimming from three to four, and after tea I shall take a brisk walk with the dogs.

MONICA (*replacing the papers on the table*) You must love exercise.

CONSTANCE. Love it? I loathe it!

MONICA. Then why bother?

CONSTANCE. It's the only way.

MONICA. To what?

Constance (*turning to the sofa*) Keep my figure. (*With her back to the audience, she bends and places a cushion in position on the sofa*)

Monica. How typically British.

Constance (*turning*) Taking exercise? (*She moves* R *and takes a golf club from a golf bag against the wall* R)

Monica. Taking extreme measures to preserve something which no longer exists. (*She puts her brief-case on the table* C)

Constance. Monica.

Monica. The sort of measures, in fact, that we used to expect from men. Measures with whiskers on them.

Constance. Well, we can't abolish all the male habits. I'm far too fond of golf to do that. (*She practises a few swings*)

Monica. But as our first woman Prime Minister, you are expected to be more original.

Constance. Perhaps. (*She lines up meticulously for a vital putt*)

Monica (*huffily*) Shall I remove the flag?

Constance. Dear Monica! (*She hands Monica the club*)

Monica. Thank you.

Constance. But as to being original—well, I am.

Monica (*crossing above the sofa to* R) The First Lord of the Admiralty has another word for it. (*She replaces the club in the golf bag*)

Constance. Helen Marchbanks?

Monica (*crossing to* C) She's never forgiven you.

Constance. What for?

Monica (*turning to Constance*) Giving her an obsolete ministry.

Constance (*crossing to* LC) Trouble is she won't admit it is obsolete.

Monica. Exactly.

Constance. Criticizing.

Monica. Constantly.

Constance. Votes of censure. Arguments. Jealousies.

Monica (*moving to* R *of the table* C) She can't forget she was an M.P. when there were men around.

Constance. I don't know how they stood her. Poor devils.

Monica. She's after your job, you know.

Constance. What!

Monica. I'm sure of it.

Constance. That settles it. I'll have her political scalp if it's the last thing I do.

Monica. It won't be the last, P.M. It'll be the next.

Constance. The next?

Monica. Tomorrow's Defence debate. (*She picks up some papers from the table* C *and hands them to Constance*) Your *coup de grâce*.

Constance. What's this?

Monica. Your speech for tomorrow.

Constance. Is this what you wanted me for?

Monica. Yes.

Constance. But you showed me the draft last Thursday. (*She returns the papers to Monica*)

MONICA. This isn't that draft. This is a re-drafted draft. (*She returns the papers to Constance*)

CONSTANCE. Can't it wait? I shan't speak until the afternoon. I could have run over the amendments over lunch.

MONICA. You'd have had indigestion.

CONSTANCE. They must be drastic.

MONICA. Rather.

CONSTANCE. What are they?

MONICA. The abolition of the three armed services.

CONSTANCE. That's unthinkable! (*She hands the papers to Monica*)

MONICA. But original. (*She puts the papers on the table* C) Try and forget your husband was a general.

CONSTANCE (*crossing to the sofa and sitting*) That has nothing to do with it. Monica, in my brief tenure of office, we have not stood still. Food production, under my guiding hand, has risen to thirty per cent of its old level. The telephone service is almost back to its former state of inefficiency. True, there are no buses, no trains, but even in this I see a blessing—the return, to its former place in the economy, of the horse. Yes, I think I can say that since I was elected to power . . .

MONICA. By a majority of one.

CONSTANCE. Since I was elected to power, we have advanced. But abolish the Army? Never.

MONICA. We don't need an army. There's no-one to fight. And as for the Navy, how many of our sailors know the prow from the poop? However, the most important aspect of the proposal seems to have escaped you.

CONSTANCE. What's that?

MONICA. The vacancies it will create.

CONSTANCE. Vacancies?

MONICA. In your Cabinet.

CONSTANCE. Monica! You're a genius.

MONICA. No Navy—no First Lord.

CONSTANCE. No First Lord—no Marchbanks. Brilliant!

MONICA. Not at all.

CONSTANCE. It's so good it's a wonder I didn't think of it myself.

MONICA. Not really.

CONSTANCE. I can just see her face. She'll burst. She'll bloody well burst.

MONICA. She was near it last month, when we debated the economy cuts.

CONSTANCE. I put her in her place then all right. You heard my speech?

MONICA. I wrote it. (*She picks up the papers and hands them to Constance*)

CONSTANCE. Oh, yes, of course. Well, I'll go through this immediately. How long is it?

MONICA. Eight double foolscaps and a demi-quarto.

CONSTANCE. Far too much. There's supposed to be a paper shortage.

MONICA. I typed it on the back of your last one.

CONSTANCE. Oh, I see. Good girl. Got to set an example.

(*There is a tap on the door* L)

(*She calls*) Come in.

(DORA *enters* L. *She is dressed as a butler*)

Oh, it's you, Dora. Why did you knock?

DORA. To get in, of course.

CONSTANCE. I've told you before, butlers do not knock. They just glide in.

DORA. Glide in? (*She indicates her trousers*) In these?

CONSTANCE (*rising*) It's not difficult. An imperceptible movement of the feet. (*She demonstrates*) Remember how Jenkins used to do it? Poor Jenkins.

(*All three, at the mention of Jenkins, bow their heads in unison and stand for a few seconds in attitudes of respectful attention*)

DORA. Well, if you're not satisfied, I'll go back to being a maid.

CONSTANCE. You'll do no such thing. You're a butler now, so you'll jolly well buttle.

DORA. Oh, I will, will I?

CONSTANCE. You will—and in those trousers. There's an acute clothing shortage.

(DORA *moves to the door* L *and turns*)

DORA. Ever thought about me giving notice?

CONSTANCE. You can't.

MONICA. Control of Labour Act. Section thirty-nine.

CONSTANCE. Exactly.

DORA. You know what you can do with that.

CONSTANCE. I beg your pardon?

DORA. Up your ruddy 'Ouse of Commons.

(DORA *exits* L. MONICA *moves to the door* L *and closes it*)

CONSTANCE (*sitting on the sofa*) It's no good. I can't stand her impertinence much longer.

MONICA. Give her a chance. Insolence is the only outlet the poor thing has these days.

CONSTANCE. I suppose so.

MONICA (*moving* C) I wonder what she wanted.

CONSTANCE (*rising*) Wanted? Oh, my God! (*She moves to the bell-push up* R *and presses it*) And heaven help her if she knocks this time.

(*There is a tap on the door* L)

The half-witted little . . . (*She calls*) Come in. (*She moves below the sofa*)

(DORA *enters* L)

DORA (*in an affected voice*) You rang, madam?

CONSTANCE. What did you come in for just now?

DORA. Lydia Parker's here.

CONSTANCE. You mean "The Minister of Science".

DORA. Do I? I wouldn't know. With all these Cabinet re-shuffles it's hard to remember who does what. Shall I send her in?

CONSTANCE. No, Dora. Show her in.

DORA. Blimey, you'd think she didn't know the way. She was only here last Tuesday.

(DORA *exits* L)

CONSTANCE. Now what does Lydia want?

MONICA (*picking up her brief-case*) The last I heard she was off to Aldermaston to see if she could pick up some useful equipment. (*She moves to the french windows*)

CONSTANCE. Perhaps she has.

(DORA *enters* L *and stands above the doorway*)

DORA (*announcing*) The Right *H*onourable Lydia Parker, M.P. and Bar.

(LYDIA PARKER *enters* L *and looks curiously at Dora.* DORA *bows low and exits* L, *closing the door behind her*)

LYDIA (*crossing to* C) Whatever is the matter with Dora? Has she been at your cellar?

CONSTANCE. I hope not. She's been behaving peculiarly, I admit. Makes one wonder whether she hasn't found a man. (*She sits on the sofa*)

LYDIA (*moving to* L *of the sofa; sharply*) What made you say that?

CONSTANCE. Say what?

LYDIA. About Dora finding a man.

CONSTANCE. Nothing. Just a figure of speech. (*She laughs*) Why? Have you found one?

LYDIA. No.

CONSTANCE. I thought not.

LYDIA. As a matter of fact—(*she pauses dramatically*) I've found two.

(MONICA *and* CONSTANCE *look at Lydia with surprise and interest.* MONICA *decides to dismiss the remark as a flippancy*)

MONICA (*moving down* LC) Joking aside, Lydia, what did you want to see us about?

LYDIA. Have you got a drink? (*She smiles, enjoying her moment*)

CONSTANCE (*rising*) I'll ring for Dora. No, on second thoughts, I won't. Sherry's far too scarce to be spilled over the carpet. (*She resumes her seat*) Can you cope, Monica?

MONICA. Of course. Medium dry, or medium sweet? (*She puts her brief-case on the table* C)

LYDIA. Is there any difference?

MONICA. None. (*She moves to the sideboard*)

LYDIA (*moving above the table* C) Then I'll have a gin and tonic.

(MONICA *pours drinks*)

CONSTANCE. Lemon juice for me. Good for the figure. Though Monica claims that doesn't matter any more.

LYDIA. But it might matter again. That's what I've come to see you about.

MONICA. We thought you were at Aldermaston.

LYDIA. I was. I've just come from there.

CONSTANCE. Did you find anything useful?

LYDIA. Extremely useful—in a manner of speaking.

CONSTANCE (*rising*) You're holding something back. (*She moves to* R *of the table* C) Out with it.

MONICA. Yes, I detect a note of suppressed excitement in her manner.

CONSTANCE. Nonsense! She's as cool as a cucumber.

MONICA. Only on the surface—underneath she's on fire. (*She picks up drinks for Lydia and Constance and moves to* L *of the table* C)

LYDIA. Tell me—have you heard of the "Van Allen Belt"?

CONSTANCE. Monica, have I heard of the Van Allen Belt? (*She takes her drink from Monica*)

MONICA. I think so. It's a radio-active area up in the stratosphere, isn't it? (*She hands Lydia her drink*)

LYDIA. More or less. Well, down at Aldermaston—before the catastrophe——

(*They all bow their heads in unison*)

—they were examining the effects of the Van Allen Belt on men.

CONSTANCE. How?

LYDIA. They duplicated the conditions underground. In the middle they put a space capsule. It was sheathed in a new, experimental type of insulation.

MONICA. And inside the capsule?

LYDIA. They put two men. I found them this morning.

(*There is a pause*)

CONSTANCE. And?

LYDIA. What do you mean—"and"?

CONSTANCE. And what?

LYDIA. Well, isn't that enough?

CONSTANCE. To what?

LYDIA. To flabbergast you?

CONSTANCE. It takes more than a couple of corpses to flabbergast me. (*She moves below the sofa*)

LYDIA. Corpses? These two weren't corpses. They were alive.

(*There is a stunned silence.* CONSTANCE *sits on the sofa*)

CONSTANCE. I can't believe it. It's impossible. It's downright . . .

MONICA (*crossing to* L *of the sofa and turning to Lydia*) You say these men were specially protected?

LYDIA. Yes. And locked in from the outside.

Monica. Then the protection would have worked against the Thing.

Lydia. It did.

Constance. But what have they lived on all this time?

Lydia. Dope and hope.

Constance. What do you mean?

Lydia. Vitamin pills and yoga. At least I suppose it was yoga. I found one in a cross-legged stupor, contemplating his navel. The other was in a state of suspended animation.

Constance. But this is sensational. (*She rises and hands her glass to Monica*)

Monica. It's a miracle! (*She takes Lydia's glass and crosses to the sideboard*)

Constance. Just a minute. When they're brought to the surface —they'll die.

Lydia. No. I tested the atmosphere. The Q factor's disappeared.

Constance (*looking reprovingly at Monica*) Really? Why didn't someone tell me? When?

Lydia. Probably ages ago.

Monica. When are you going to bring them out.

Lydia. I've already done so.

Constance. What!

Lydia. I rang that W.R.A.C. major from Security. She's bringing them down in an ambulance.

Monica. Where?

Lydia. Here.

Constance. You can't.

Lydia (*moving to the french windows*) I could hardly leave them where they were.

Monica. I should think not. If this news leaked out we'd have the biggest Aldermaston March ever.

Constance. But here! (*She sits on the sofa*)

Lydia. Why not?

Constance. They'll—they'll frighten the grouse.

Monica. I think it's ideal. We'll have to keep an eye on them.

Lydia. Politically speaking, they're dynamite.

Monica. And biologically speaking, dynamite is an understatement. (*She declaims*) Prime Minister, this is the biggest thing since Adam. We've cornered the market.

Constance. Yes, but what in?

Monica. It's magnificent!

Constance. Personally, I don't like it.

Monica. At your age you don't have to. Lydia, what time do you expect them?

Lydia (*moving above the table* c) Any moment.

Monica (*taking charge*) Who knows about this?

Lydia. The Major, and the Major's driver.

Monica. Good. What about the servants?

Constance. There's only Dora.

Lydia. You'll have to send her away.

CONSTANCE. And do the washing-up ourselves?

LYDIA. What else?

MONICA. Let her into the secret.

LYDIA. Join the Board?

MONICA. She won't give us away. She'll realize the fewer the shareholders, the larger the dividend.

(CONSTANCE *nods approvingly*)

CONSTANCE (*rising*) I'll ring for her. (*She moves* R *and presses the bell-push*)

MONICA. Well, Lydia, this is certainly a bombshell you've dropped on us. (*She pours three drinks*)

CONSTANCE. And the implications are so breath-taking, I can't talk about them.

(CONSTANCE *and* LYDIA *stroll down* R *and back again as though in the lobby of the House of Commons*)

LYDIA. As a politician, you have to

CONSTANCE. You're a politician yourself.

LYDIA. In name only. You roped me in because there was nobody else.

CONSTANCE. Nonsense! You must have been one of our finest all-round boffins, even when there were men. What are these two like?

LYDIA (*with distaste*) The conscious one is some sort of R.A.F. officer.

CONSTANCE. You don't care for him?

(CONSTANCE *and* LYDIA *cross down* L)

LYDIA. Judge for yourself. (*Her face lights up*) The unconscious one is a scientist. But even in his sleep every inch an Alpha Plus.

MONICA. That's something. Let's celebrate. (*She hands drinks to Constance and Lydia then takes her own drink and stands above the table* C)

LYDIA. I don't know the approved method of reviving him, but his friend says he can cope. (*She crosses to the sofa*)

(DORA *enters* L)

CONSTANCE. Dora, why didn't you knock?

DORA. Gor blimey! You just told me not to.

CONSTANCE. So I did. Well, try breaking it off gradually.

DORA. Anyone'd think you was talking about an engagement.

CONSTANCE (*crossing to* R *of the sofa*) Dora, I want you to prepare yourself for a shock.

DORA (*moving* C) Nothing shocks me. Remember that night when the general came out of the bathroom without . . .

CONSTANCE (*turning to Dora*) Not that kind of a shock.

DORA. Is there any other.

CONSTANCE. Of course.

DORA. Go on, then.

CONSTANCE. A lot of what I have to say is highly scientific.

(DORA *looks somewhat vacuous and moves below the sofa*)

So I won't bother. The fact is, I have found, or perhaps I should say, unearthed, two live men. They'll be here in a few minutes.

(DORA *swoons on the sofa*)

There, I knew she couldn't take it. (*To Lydia*) Help me bring her round.

(*They place* DORA *in a sitting position and gently slap her face*)

Dora! Wake up.

(DORA *wakes*)

DORA. Oh! (*She rises*) For a moment I thought you said you'd found two live men.
LYDIA. We have.

(DORA *swoons again on to the sofa*)

CONSTANCE. What did you have to say that for?

(*Once again they slap* DORA *into wakefulness*)

DORA. You did say—men?
CONSTANCE. That's right.
DORA. Two men?
CONSTANCE. Yes.
DORA. Alive?
CONSTANCE. Very much so.
DORA. And coming here?
MONICA. Yes.
DORA. Cor! (*A thought strikes her*) How old?
LYDIA. Old enough.
DORA. Cor!
CONSTANCE. Stop crowing and pull yourself together.
DORA (*rising*) I'm all there now.
CONSTANCE. Good. We're relying on you to behave yourself.
DORA (*crossing to* L) What, with two . . . I mean, haven't I always?
CONSTANCE. Only since the lads of the village—departed.

(*They all bow their heads again in unison*)

DORA. Anyone'd think I was fast . . .
CONSTANCE. And loose.

(*The sound of a car arriving and stopping is heard*)

LYDIA. That will be the ambulance.

(*They all readjust their hair and make-up.* DORA *rushes to the door* L)

CONSTANCE. Where are you going, Dora?
DORA. To buttle, of course.

(DORA *exits* L.

LYDIA *follows her off, leaving the door ajar*)

CONSTANCE. Monica, this is—quite a moment.
MONICA. A milestone in history.
CONSTANCE. Something we never thought we'd see again. The new dawn——
MONICA. —of Man.
CONSTANCE. It seems so long ago, I hardly know how to receive them.
MONICA. Casually and calmly, but with dignity.
CONSTANCE. Dignity? We must treat them with respect.
MONICA. And moderate our language in their presence. But they must be left in no doubt as to which is the dominant sex from now on.

(WING COMMANDER NIGEL LAWLER *enters* L, *carrying* DORA *in his arms. She is stiffly unconscious.* NIGEL *wears an R.A.F. uniform and seems very pleased with himself*)

NIGEL. I found this in the hall. Does it belong to either of you?
MONICA. Not again! Put her on the sofa.

(NIGEL *lays Dora rigidly on the sofa.* CONSTANCE *and* MONICA *stand above the* sofa. CONSTANCE *is* R *of Monica*)

NIGEL. She seems to be suffering from something. (*He stands* L *of the sofa*)
MONICA. Evidently *rigor mortis.*

(LYDIA *enters* L)

NIGEL. Either that or she's sloshed.
MONICA. If you mean inebriated, the answer is "no". She is merely overawed.
NIGEL. Overawed?
MONICA. By you.
NIGEL. I'm most gratified.
MONICA. After all, you're one of the two most attractive men in the world.
NIGEL (*indicating Lydia*) So this ravishing creature's been telling me.
LYDIA. Don't call me a ravishing creature.
NIGEL. I know it sounds ridiculous, but remember I've been "without" as long as you have. By the way, the name's Nigel Lawler, Wing Commander, R.A.F.
MONICA (*indicating Constance*) This is the Prime Minister. I'm her P.P.S.
NIGEL. She doesn't look much like a Prime Minister. Quite a different shape from the last one.
CONSTANCE. Shape? (*She moves down* R)
NIGEL. Good thing on the whole, I suppose. Gives the cartoonists a break.
CONSTANCE. Really! (*She turns her back on Nigel in disgust*)

(Nigel *views Constance's hind quarters with good-humoured distaste*)

Nigel. And now that we're face to face I've got an important question to ask you.
Constance (*turning*) Well?
Nigel. What about my back pay?
Constance. I beg your pardon?

(Nigel *takes a piece of card from his pocket*)

Nigel. My arithmetic isn't so hot, but I reckon it's about—(*he reads*) two thousand, seven hundred and forty-three pounds, nine shillings and tenpence.
Monica. That seems rather a lot.
Nigel. Special Aldermaston rates. We made a bomb.
Constance (*contemptuously*) Back pay! All he can think about is back pay.
Nigel. Well, I've never had so many women to spend it on. What is the female population of this country?
Monica. Twenty-six million, five hundred and twenty-five thousand and four.
Nigel. Present company excepted, that leaves a nice round figure to split with David. Let me see now—three hundred and sixty-five days in the year—with night work—shift work . . . I told you my arithmetic wasn't very good.
Monica. I shouldn't bother to calculate. Your back pay won't stretch that far. And neither will you for that matter, unless your name happens to be Methuselah.
Constance. Where is your colleague?
Nigel. Outside on the stretcher.
Constance. Conscious?
Nigel. Not yet. (*He crosses to the easy chair* R) I left the major galloping up the steps with him. Go and give her a hand, somebody. (*He lolls in the easy chair*)
Constance. What's wrong with you?
Nigel. Nothing. That's why I can't oblige. I want to stay that way. You wouldn't want to rupture half the country's assets, now, would you?
Lydia. I'm beginning to wonder whether we shouldn't have liquidated them.

(Lydia *exits* L)

Nigel (*rising and moving to Constance*) Hope springs eternal . . . Nice place you've got here. What happened to Number Ten?
Constance. It's been turned into a national monument.
Nigel. Couldn't stand the smell of tobacco?
Constance. We've made many changes.
Nigel. You've kept the Upper House?
Constance. Naturally.
Nigel. Still call it the Lords?

(Constance *looks shocked*)

CONSTANCE. We couldn't very well call it the Ladies, now could we?

NIGEL. You could, but it might have led to complications.

MONICA (*moving down* L; *looking a little worried*) Wing Commander, is your friend anything like you?

NIGEL. I'm sorry to say——

MONICA. He is?

NIGEL. —not in the least. (*He crosses to the sideboard*)

CONSTANCE. Thank God!

(NIGEL *helps himself to a drink*)

NIGEL. David's as innocent as a new-born lamb, and fifteen times as intelligent. He's a non-drinker, non-smoker, and non- . . . (*He breaks off and listens*) That sounds like his trolley.

(LYDIA *enters* L *and stands to one side.*

MAJOR DANVERS-BISHOP, W.R.A.C., *follows Lydia on, wheeling a hospital trolley. On it sleeps* PROFESSOR DAVID MOXTON. *A typical hospital intraveneous feeding device is attached to the trolley*)

MAJOR (*saluting*) Major Danvers-Bishop reporting with recumbent astronaut.

LYDIA (*pushing the trolley to* C) This is Professor David Moxton.

NIGEL. Looking absolutely angelic. Seems a pity to wake him.

CONSTANCE. I fail to see why you haven't done so before.

NIGEL. Couldn't tackle it on an empty stomach. Now I've had a kip in the ambulance and a drink, I'll have a bash. Did you bring that kit, Major?

MAJOR (*producing a box from under the trolley*) Astronaut Reviving Kit, Mark Two, with padlock.

NIGEL. And the key?

MAJOR. Key?

NIGEL. For opening the padlock.

MAJOR. It must be in the ambulance. I'll go and see.

(*The* MAJOR *exits* L)

NIGEL. In the meantime we'll try the corkscrew. (*He collects the corkscrew from the sideboard and attacks the padlock*)

(CONSTANCE *and* LYDIA *inspect David*)

CONSTANCE. He doesn't look much.

LYDIA. We can fatten him up.

CONSTANCE. We can try. But there's not much you can do when the basic material isn't there.

LYDIA (*indicating Nigel*) There's always him.

CONSTANCE. Humph! I don't fancy a human race with him as an ancestor.

NIGEL. Why not? I'd make a damn fine ancestor.

CONSTANCE. Young man, whatever else you may be, you are not a gentleman. Personally, I regard breeding as extremely important.

NIGEL. I rather enjoy it myself. (*He opens the box*) There we are.

Constance. Furthermore, if the choice were mine, I wouldn't have you fathering the next generation of Englishmen if you were the last man on earth.

(Nigel *takes a hypodermic syringe and a bottle from the box and puts the box on the table* c)

Nigel. Well, if this doesn't work I jolly well will be. Ah, yes. Reviving fluid.

Lydia (*moving to Nigel*) May I see? Out of professional curiosity.

Nigel. Certainly. It's wonderful stuff. Works in ninety seconds, by revitalizing the brain, breathing and blood count.

(Lydia *peers closely at the bottle*)

(*Confidentially*) I can recommend it for a hot date. Over to you. (*He gives the syringe and bottle to Lydia*)

Lydia. How much?

Nigel. Two c.c.s in the left arm.

(Lydia *administers the injection.* Dora *groans*)

What do you know? (*He moves to the sofa*) The Sleeping Beauty's waking up in sympathy. (*He gently slaps Dora's cheeks*) Wake up.

(Dora *wakes and sees Nigel*)

Dora. Cor!

(Dora *smothers* Nigel *in an embrace and pulls him on to the sofa with her, causing him to somersault over the back of the sofa.* Dora *swoons again*)

Lydia (*putting the syringe and bottle in the box and moving to the sofa*) Perhaps if I took over she'd revive quicker. (*She attends to Dora*)

(Nigel *rises*)

Dora (*waking*) Where's he gone? What happened?

Nigel. You passed out. You're the first woman who's ever done that with me. I'll make you president of my fan club.

Dora. Cor!

Monica. All right, Dora. That's enough drooling for the moment. The Wing Commander's head is big enough as it is.

Lydia (*standing over David*) He's stirring.

Nigel. I think the first face he ought to see is mine. We don't want to scare him to death. Come on, old boy. Time to get up. (*To Monica*) Glass of sherry, quick.

(Monica *quickly pours a little sherry into a glass and hands it to Nigel*)

It's probably against the blighter's religion, but here goes. (*He pours a little sherry into David's mouth*) Drink it down, that's it. Sit up now. (*He eases David into a sitting position*) Now open your eyes.

(David *sits up, opens his eyes and looks at Nigel*)

DAVID (*distastefully*) Urgh!
NIGEL (*happily*) He recognized me.
DAVID. Where am I?
NIGEL. Among friends.
DAVID. What is that appalling taste in my mouth?
NIGEL. Sherry.
DAVID. Nigel, you know my views on the artificial stimulation of the nervous system through alcohol.
NIGEL. Glad to see you're your usual self.
DAVID. Who are these ladies?
NIGEL. Reading from left to right—the Prime Minister, her P.P.S., the Minister of Science and the upstairs maid.
DORA (*rising; indignantly*) Butler.
DAVID. This is either an hallucination or a dream. (*He gets down from the trolley*)
MONICA. It's neither. (*She takes a paper from her brief-case*)
NIGEL. Shall I pinch you?
DORA. That's a smashing idea. I know just the place.
CONSTANCE (*moving above the sofa*) Dora! Go and help the Major search the ambulance.
DORA. Don't tell me there's a third hanging round that you've gone and mislaid.
CONSTANCE. The search is for a key.
DORA. Key?
NIGEL. But . . .
CONSTANCE. A most important key.
DORA. Oh, all right. But keep an eye on these two while I'm gone. After all, this is a democracy. Fair shares for all.

(DORA *crosses and exits* L)

DAVID. I'm going mad. The penalty of genius. It happened to Newton, it happened to . . .
NIGEL. Now, take it easy, Professor. You are every bit as sane as I am.
DAVID. That's no consolation. What I need is an explanation.
NIGEL. You'll get one. Even if it means publishing a White Paper.
MONICA. We have. (*She hands the paper to David*)
NIGEL. She doesn't miss a trick, does she?
MONICA. It's rather brief, but there's a paper shortage.
LYDIA. You should know. You caused it.
DAVID. And does this explain the—er—somewhat peculiar circumstances attending my regeneration?
NIGEL. The basic facts are simple.
DAVID. Namely?
NIGEL. One: you and I are the only men left alive.
DAVID. In the world?
MONICA. Yes.
DAVID. But how?
NIGEL. We were in our little nest, protected from radiation,

when somebody let off some new super-duper explosive whatsit which back-fired . . .

Monica. And killed off all the men.

Nigel. Except us. (*He claps a hand on David's shoulder*) My boy, a great responsibility has fallen on your shoulders.

David. True. We'll need all the scientists we can get. What about the women?

Nigel. They escaped.

David. How?

Nigel (*to Lydia*) You tell him, sweetheart.

(Lydia *recites at an almost inhuman pace, while* David *indicates by occasionally nodding and humming that he follows perfectly*)

Lydia. The high temperature stresses generated by the device created an abnormally high excitation factor. This led to an unsuspected fusion of the Theta particles and the emission of a discharge—the Q Factor—which caused rapid decomposition of the male chromosomes but left the female chromosomes intact. It's all in the White Paper.

David. But how extraordinarily interesting. Now where are my glasses (*He takes his glasses from his pocket and puts them on*) Ah, here they are. I assume this discharge has disappeared. (*He moves and sits on the sofa at the left end of it*)

Nigel. Yes, old boy. We've reached the end of the queue.

(David *reads and studies the paper*)

Now, while the infant prodigy gets absorbed in his homework, perhaps you can explain something to me.

Monica. We'll do our best.

Nigel. How are we going to operate?

Constance. Operate?

Nigel. David and I.

Constance (*crossing to Nigel*) I don't follow you.

Nigel. I sincerely hope you won't.

Constance. Would you mind . . . ?

Nigel (*nudging Constance*) Come now, P.M., don't be coy.

(Constance *looks at Nigel in disgust*)

You know as much about the birds and the bees as I do.

Constance (*crossing down* R) That I doubt.

Nigel. I take it the two of us are going to be pretty busy from now on, one way and . . .

Monica. Another?

Nigel. Exactly. And what I want to know is, what's in it for me?

Constance. What had you in mind?

Nigel (*sitting on the left arm of the sofa*) Accommodation, remuneration, advance publicity—and, of course—transport.

Monica. Transport is difficult.

Nigel. You can't expect us to flit round the country on a tandem.

MONICA. We don't expect you to flit round the country at all.
NIGEL. Mountains coming to Mahomet, eh?
MONICA. For one thing there's an acute petrol shortage.
CONSTANCE (*crossing to Monica*) For another the Government has no power to supply you with a vehicle.

(CONSTANCE *and* MONICA *stand together, as if to express unity*)

MONICA. Not quite correct.
CONSTANCE. No?
MONICA. Under the National Health Act we could run to an invalid-carriage.
CONSTANCE. Which would hardly be appropriate.
MONICA. Yet.
NIGEL. Just a moment. In my day, V.I.P.s went about in Rolls Royces.
CONSTANCE. But you aren't going to go about at all.
LYDIA. You're far too valuable.
MONICA. You need protection.
NIGEL. I need protection like an Arab needs an umbrella. (*He rises*) I'm off. And if you won't give me a car, I'll go it on foot. Coming, David?
DAVID (*engrossed in the paper*) Eh?
CONSTANCE. You're both Government property. And until we decide what to do with you, you'll remain here.
MONICA. Under protective custody.
NIGEL. We won't stand for this. Will we, David?
DAVID. Stand for what, old boy?
NIGEL. Didn't you hear what she said?
DAVID. No, and I do wish you wouldn't interrupt. This is absolutely fascinating.
NIGEL. Look! These petticoat politicians say we've got to stay here.
DAVID. Well, it appears to be reasonably congenial.
NIGEL. Congenial!
DAVID. Do watch your adrenaline secretions.
NIGEL. In other words, we're prisoners.
DAVID. Who?
NIGEL. Us.
DAVID. Oh. (*He resumes his reading*)
NIGEL. Ladies, you can have *him*. (*He crosses to the door* L) My country needs me. I'm off. (*He opens the door*)

(*The* MAJOR, *holding a gun, is outside the door and menacingly bars Nigel's path*)

LYDIA. Don't underestimate the Major. She's a first-class shot.
NIGEL. She wouldn't dare.
CONSTANCE. If the need arises, the Government will adopt a strong policy.
MONICA. Scorched earth.
NIGEL. Now, be reasonable.

(*The sound of dogs barking is heard off*)

MONICA (*moving to the french windows*) And apart from the Major, we have the dogs.

CONSTANCE. These premises are guarded by a pack of Alsatians.

MONICA. Half an hour's training and we'll have them going for anything in trousers.

CONSTANCE. You have that in hand, Major?

MAJOR. Corporal Forster's with them now, Prime Minister. This afternoon we'll supplement their numbers with one or two other breeds—specially trained.

CONSTANCE. Good show! Splendid initiative.

(DORA *enters* L. *She is now without her trousers and is wearing a frilly pair of briefs. She stands to one side of the door and blows a boatswain's whistle*)

Dora!

DORA. What?

CONSTANCE. Your trousers!

DORA. I can't see no trousers.

CONSTANCE. Where are they?

DORA. I lent 'em to Corporal Forster to train the dogs. (*She blows her whistle*)

CONSTANCE. Stop making that ridiculous noise.

DORA. I'm piping the Admiral aboard.

CONSTANCE. The Admiral?

MONICA. Helen Marchbanks?

DORA. 'S right.

MONICA. Here?

DORA. In the hall. Taking off her coat.

CONSTANCE. Monica. Do something.

MONICA. Major! Get them out of here.

MAJOR (*crossing to the sofa*) Come on, you two. Through there. (*She indicates the door* R)

NIGEL (*crossing to* C) Now look here, I'll . . .

(*The* MAJOR *sticks her gun in Nigel's middle*)

(*Hastily*) I'll just pop in here for a while.

(NIGEL *crosses and exits* R)

MAJOR (*to David*) And you.

DAVID (*rising*) Really! I deplore violence.

(DAVID *exits* R.
*The* MAJOR *follows him off*)

CONSTANCE. If Marchbanks finds out . . .

MONICA. Leave her to me. And keep cool.

(*They adopt attitudes of relaxed innocence.* DORA *stands to attention and stops piping.* LYDIA *and* CONSTANCE *sit on the sofa,* LYDIA R *of*

*Constance.* MONICA *takes out a notebook and pencil and stands above the sofa*)

DORA (*announcing*) The First Lord of the Admiralty.

(HELEN MARCHBANKS, W.R.N.S., the *First Lord of the Admiralty, enters* L. *She is in uniform. Without looking at Dora* HELEN *points at Dora's legs*)

HELEN. Improperly dressed. (*She crosses to* C) Hello, Connie. Monica. Just popped in on my way to town.

(DORA *exits* L *and closes the door behind her*)

MONICA. Rather a circular route, wasn't it?
HELEN. You too, Lydia? What's this? A Cabinet meeting?
LYDIA (*rising and moving down* R) Hardly.
HELEN. Not without me, eh?
MONICA. Lydia's visit is social. What's yours?
HELEN (*seeing the trolley*) Great Scott! What's this?
LYDIA. An intravenous feeding device.
HELEN. Prefer eggs and bacon meself. What are you doing with it?
MONICA. It's a military secret.
HELEN. Naval?
MONICA (*moving above the table* C) No, purely Air Force. (*She pushes the trolley up* L)
HELEN. We don't have an Air Force.
CONSTANCE. If it comes to that we don't have a Navy.
HELEN. Rubbish! Just come down from Pompey. Reviewing the Fleet.
CONSTANCE. Was it all there?
HELEN. Funny you should say that. I seem to have lost three cruisers and a submarine.
MONICA. Have you tried the bath?
HELEN. No.
MONICA. Or the Navy files?
HELEN. At the Admiralty?
MONICA. No, the Russian Embassy.
HELEN. You be careful what you say, Monica.
MONICA. Aren't I always?
HELEN. I'll come straight to the point. Connie, I want something.
CONSTANCE. Yes?
HELEN. Your job.
CONSTANCE (*rising*) You?
HELEN. This country needs a leader. You're just a figurehead.
CONSTANCE. That is a matter of opinion.
HELEN. It's a lot of people's opinion.
MONICA. Whose?
HELEN. Six of the Cabinet, to start with.
CONSTANCE. I don't believe it.

HELEN. You will at tomorrow's debate. We'll split the Government in two.

CONSTANCE. Tomorrow's debate, eh? You just wait till you hear tomorrow's debate, that's all.

MONICA (*anxiously*) P.M.!

CONSTANCE. Tomorrow, my dear Admiral, we are going to abolish the Navy.

HELEN. Rubbish!

CONSTANCE. Scuttled! That's what you'll be.

HELEN. Unless of course we scuttle you first. Your stock's pretty low at the moment. Don't be surprised if you find yourself out of office and me in. I've an ace or two up my sleeve, I can tell you.

CONSTANCE. You've nothing up your sleeve but tattoo marks.

HELEN. Wait and see. That's all. And watch out for the aces.

(HELEN *crosses and exits* L)

CONSTANCE (*calling after her*) No need. I hold two trumps. Cabinet split, indeed. Just wait till I produce my men. Bring them in. I want to look at them.

MONICA (*crossing to the door* R) Again?

CONSTANCE. Again.

MONICA (*opening the door and calling*) You can come out now.

(*The* MAJOR, NIGEL *and* DAVID *enter* L. DAVID, *still reading, crosses to the sofa and sits, never taking his eyes from the paper*)

NIGEL. I warn you, I intend to write to my M.P. about this.

MONICA. Quiet, please. Satisfied, P.M.?

CONSTANCE. They may not be much, but they're mine. Let's retire and discuss tactics. Major, you're in charge. If there's any trouble, blow your whistle. (*She crosses to the door* L) Monica! Lydia!

(CONSTANCE, *trying to give the appearance of possessing great powers of leadership, ushers* MONICA *and* LYDIA *off* L, *then follows them off.* NIGEL *sits* R *of David on the sofa. The* MAJOR *moves and stands up* C)

NIGEL. Well, now we know where we stand.

DAVID (*pendantically*) Sit.

NIGEL. For heaven's sake get your nose out of that thing and face facts.

DAVID. These are facts. Intriguing and absorbing facts.

NIGEL. More absorbing than the fact that you and I are being held prisoners?

DAVID. Prisoners?

NIGEL. By a gaggle of sex-starved tabbies.

MAJOR. Now, then! Now, then!

NIGEL. Quiet, you! And say "sir" when you address a superior officer.

MAJOR. Say what?

NIGEL. "Sir." (*To David*) Consider the implications. Imagine yourself being caught in the coal-shed by one of those fly-blown females. Think of it.

DAVID (*suddenly alarmed*) Oh, my God! (*He rises*)

NIGEL. Can't you feel it? Their lecherous breath on your neck—their clammy claws on your . . . (*He rises and clutches David*)

DAVID. Collar?

NIGEL. Each with the touch of a sex-starved sea-lion.

DAVID. What do we do?

NIGEL. Do? (*He whispers*) We get the hell out of here.

MAJOR. What was that?

NIGEL. Sir!

MAJOR. Sir. (*She springs to attention*)

NIGEL. I said I wouldn't say "no" to a bottle of beer.

MAJOR. There isn't any—sir.

NIGEL. Too bad. (*He wanders up* L, *wondering how to disarm the Major*)

MAJOR. I've got my eye on you—sir.

(NIGEL *picks up a large Chinese vase from the table up* L, *visualizing it as a weapon*)

Both eyes.

NIGEL (*indicating the vase; with a feeble laugh*) Ming. (*He replaces the vase, looks out of the french windows and feigns sudden alarm*) My God! The enemy!

(DAVID *and the* MAJOR *rush to the french windows and look out.* NIGEL *swiftly seizes the Major's gun*)

MAJOR (*yelling*) Hel . . . !

(NIGEL *jabs the Major with the gun and silences her*)

NIGEL. Gag her.

DAVID. Eh?

NIGEL. Gag her.

DAVID. What with?

NIGEL. Anything. Your socks.

DAVID. I can't take off my socks in the presence of a woman.

NIGEL. You're going to be a fat lot of use to the nation, aren't you?

DAVID. What about a cushion?

NIGEL. Too small.

DAVID. Curtains?

NIGEL. Too long.

DAVID. I know. (*He takes a roll of cotton wool from the Reviving Kit*) How much?

NIGEL. Just imagine she's a cigarette lighter. And hurry.

(DAVID *tries to put some cotton wool into the Major's mouth*)

DAVID. She's clenching her teeth.

NIGEL (*jabbing the gun into the Major's back*) Say "ah".

MAJOR. Aaaah!

NIGEL. Now!

(DAVID *inserts the cotton wool and withdraws his hand in pain*)

DAVID. She bit me.
NIGEL. If you don't get a move on, the dogs'll follow suit.
DAVID. Good Lord! Rabies!
NIGEL (*giving David his handkerchief*) Use this.

(*They gag the Major*)

Then tie her hands.
DAVID. No string.
NIGEL. Use your braces.
DAVID. Now, look here . . .
NIGEL (*indicating the standard lamp*) Over there. Cord.

(DAVID *rips some cord from the shade of the standard lamp and ties the Major's hands behind her back*)

Can you run?
DAVID. No.
NIGEL. Heaven help you, then. Is she tied?
DAVID. I think so.

(NIGEL *deposits the lampshade over the Major's head. They pick her up and lay her along the sofa*)

NIGEL. Right. One, two, three—scarper!

(*They rush to the door* L. *The door opens.*
CORPORAL EVE FORSTER, W.R.A.C., *stands in the doorway, looking intensely beautiful*)

Where did you spring from?
EVE (*coming into the room*) I'm your guard.
NIGEL. Really?
EVE. I drove you down here.
NIGEL. Are you? I mean, did you?
EVE. Any objections?
NIGEL. No, no, none at all. (*Aside to David*) Untie her.
DAVID. What?
NIGEL. The Major.

(DAVID *stands still, amazed*)

Untie her. And remove her hat.
DAVID. But you just said . . .
NIGEL. Never mind what I said.

(DAVID *moves to the Major, takes off the lampshade and unties her hands*)

(*To Eve*) What's your name?
EVE. Corporal Forster.
NIGEL. Your other one.
EVE. "Eve".
NIGEL. Really.

(David *removes the Major's gag*)

Eve. What's wrong with the Major?
Nigel. Toothache. (*He twirls the gun*)
Eve. Oh, I see. (*She looks at the gun*)
Nigel. Just picked it up. It belongs to the Major. David, put this in her holster.
David (*taking the gun*) In her what?
Nigel. Holster.
David. But I thought we were going to escape.
Nigel. Escape? Who said anything about escaping? (*To Eve*) It's in the mind, you know. (*He taps his forehead*) Suspended animation. Plays tricks with the old metabolism.

(David *puts the gun in the Major's holster*)

Eve. I'm sure.
Nigel. Come over here and sit down.

(Nigel *leads* Eve *to the sofa, flicks the Major's legs to the floor, and sits, gently pulling* Eve *down beside him*)

David, get Eve a sherry. I may as well get acquainted with my new guard. By the way, the name's "Adam".

Nigel *pushes back against the* Major *who is squeezed off the sofa as—*

*the* Curtain *falls*

# ACT II

SCENE—*The same. Later that day.*

*When the* CURTAIN *rises, it is beginning to get dark and the lights are on. The record-player is playing a Highland reel.* DAVID *is seated on the sofa, engrossed in a large textbook. Outside the french windows the sound of hammering is heard and a ladder can be seen.* NIGEL *is peering out of the french windows, admiring the legs of* EVE, *who is at the top of the ladder.*

DAVID. Would you mind turning off that Gaelic cacophony. It mars my concentration.

(NIGEL *moves to the record-player and switches it off*)

Thank you.

(NIGEL *returns to the french windows. The hammering stops*)

NIGEL. You know, it shouldn't be allowed.
DAVID (*without looking up*) What?
NIGEL. Giving a job like that to a girl like Eve. She's been trying to hammer screws into the brickwork for the last half hour.
DAVID. Hammer screws?
NIGEL. With a spanner.
DAVID (*looking up*) What's she trying to fix?
NIGEL. A burglar alarm.
DAVID. Are there any, now?
NIGEL. Any what?
DAVID. Burglars.
NIGEL. Idiot! It's not to keep them out. It's to keep us in.
DAVID. I thought we'd decided not to escape.
NIGEL. They don't know that.

(*The* MAJOR *enters* L, *carrying her gun*)

Good evening, Major.
MAJOR. "Colonel", if you don't mind.
NIGEL. Colonel?
MAJOR. *Full* Colonel.
NIGEL. My God! She's been promoted.
MAJOR (*saluting*) The Prime Minister wishes me to inform you of the precautions taken to prevent your escape.
NIGEL. Fire away.

(*The* MAJOR *raises her gun*)

Er—not literally, of course.
MAJOR. All exits from this room are now fitted with burglar alarms. Any attempt to escape will set off the bells and bring me to the scene. I am a Bisley shot.

NIGEL. Congratulations.

MAJOR. What's more I shall be sleeping just across the passage.

NIGEL. You'll be quite safe.

MAJOR. Sharing my room with Corporal Forster.

NIGEL. I'll swop.

MAJOR (*crossing to the door* R) Your beds are through there in the ante-room——

(NIGEL *follows the Major to* R)

—the windows of which are also fitted with alarms. (*She crosses to* L) If you give any trouble I've a set of leg-irons.

(NIGEL *follows the Major to* L)

(*She turns*) Any questions?

NIGEL (*rising his hand*) Yes. Please may I leave the room?

MAJOR. If you follow the drill.

NIGEL. Drill?

MAJOR. You ring for the butler, who will take your message to Corporal Forster. She will inform me, and I will escort you with the assistance of George.

NIGEL. George? Who the hell's George?

MAJOR. Our new bulldog. He'll sleep in the passage.

NIGEL. I don't blame him.

MAJOR. That, then, is the drill.

NIGEL. Sounds more like a ceremonial parade.

MAJOR. I beg your pardon?

NIGEL. With regimental mascot.

MAJOR. If you've no more questions, I'll go and oil the leg-irons.

(*The* MAJOR *exits* L)

NIGEL. I hope your oil-can squeaks. (*He crosses to* R *of the sofa*) How you can sit there reading, I don't know.

DAVID. It's a book on theta radiation.

NIGEL. Lydia's?

DAVID. Naturally. We had a most rewarding discussion.

NIGEL. Yes, I reckon you've made a conquest there. Come to think of it, she's not bad in a clinical sort of way. Get her in the laboratory with a bell-jar over her head and . . .

DAVID. My interest in the lady is purely intellectual.

NIGEL. I'm well aware that your libido is about as large as a split pea. I shall have to work up enough patriotism for both of us.

DAVID. Patriotism?

NIGEL (*crossing to* C) That's what we're here for, isn't it? The P.M. called it "fathering the next generation of Englishmen". Thank goodness she doesn't know I'm Welsh.

(DORA *enters* L, *carrying a tray with two cups of tea. She is wearing a skirt and blouse*)

DORA (*moving to* L *of Nigel*) I've brought you some tea.

NIGEL. What again?

DORA. Yes.

NIGEL. You've been in and out with cups of tea all day.

DORA. Don't you like tea, then?

NIGEL. I like tea, but I don't like going for walks with bulldogs.

DORA. You've heard about George, then?

NIGEL. Yes. Do you like bulldogs, David?

DAVID (*looking up*) Bulldogs? Yes, as a matter of fact, I do, rather.

NIGEL (*taking the tray from Dora*) Give him both cups. (*He moves* RC *and hands the tray to David*) Now, Dora . . . (*He takes a step towards her*)

DORA. 'Ere! You mustn't come near me.

NIGEL. Why? Are you suffering from something?

DORA. Oh, no. Only you've got a peculiar effect on me.

NIGEL (*moving* RC) Have I now?

DORA (*with a step towards Nigel*) Ever so peculiar.

NIGEL (*retreating* R) I see.

DORA. Not that I mind.

(DAVID *puts the tray on the sofa seat beside him*)

NIGEL. No?

DORA. It's *nice* and peculiar, if you know what I mean. (*She moves to* L *of Nigel*)

NIGEL. I do. But it's too late, I'm afraid.

DORA. Why?

NIGEL. I'm half a nationalized industry.

DORA. I wish you'd let me subsidize you.

NIGEL. Try the other half. (*He points to David*) Over there, drinking tea.

DORA. Yes, but . . .

NIGEL. It would have been different a few weeks ago. Just you and I in the capsule.

DORA. And 'im.

NIGEL. He was unconscious.

DORA. Doesn't look far from it now, does he? He'd drive me clean round the 'Arpic—sitting silent like that—he would, really.

NIGEL. I had six months of it. Just him and me in the Van Allen Belt.

DORA. Cor! I bet it was tight.

NIGEL. Tight? Don't you know what the Van Allen Belt is?

DORA. 'Course I do. I seen them posters in the Tube same as everyone else, haven't I?

NIGEL. You're a Daisy, you are.

DORA (*playfully pushing him*) Go on with you! Oh! I've touched you. I've gone all queer at the knees. (*She staggers*)

(NIGEL *catches* DORA *in his arms and she quickly puts her arms around his neck*)

NIGEL. Better?

DORA (*gazing into his face*) Ever so.

(LYDIA *enters* L. *She carries a notebook and pen*)

LYDIA. Dora!
DORA (*without looking round*) Drop dead!
LYDIA. Dora! Back to the kitchen and start washing-up. The sink's piled high with tea-cups. (*She indicates some empty tea-cups on the table* C) And take these two with you.
DORA (*gazing into Nigel's face*) I only want this one.
LYDIA. Tea-cups! Come along! At once!
DORA (*turning*) Can't you mind your own business?
LYDIA. Back to the sink. And get cracking.
DORA (*moving* C) Don't worry. (*She picks up the cups from the table* C) When I handle those pots—I will.

(DORA *crosses to the door* L. NIGEL *crosses and opens the door for her.* DORA *exits* L)

NIGEL (*closing the door*) Lydia, you've no romance in your soul.
LYDIA. I've no soul. And what's more, I've no time to waste on trivialities. We've work to do.
NIGEL. Work?
LYDIA. Isn't that what you're here for?
NIGEL. I suppose so. Though I hadn't actually thought of it as work.
LYDIA (*perching on the left arm of the sofa*) Then we'll begin.
NIGEL. Begin? (*He sits on the table* C, *facing Lydia*)
LYDIA. Yes.

(*There is a pause.* NIGEL *looks at David*)

NIGEL. Here?
LYDIA. Of course.
NIGEL. You mean—now?
LYDIA. The sooner the better.
NIGEL. Oh—well—if you insist. (*He undoes his belt*)
LYDIA (*to David*) Professor Moxton, tell your friend what we want him to do.
NIGEL (*rising*) Now, look here . . .
DAVID. It's all right, Nigel—it's quite simple.
NIGEL. I know that!
DAVID (*rising*) But we must remember the genetic factors.
NIGEL. Why?
DAVID (*moving* R) In a project of such magnitude, natural selectivity . . .
NIGEL. Don't worry. Where women are concerned I'm extremely selective.
DAVID. Natural selectivity in a case like this, based on totally irrelevant factors, such as personal appearance, may fail to produce the results we desire.
LYDIA. In other words, it must be superseded by considerations of compatability.
DAVID. And intelligence.

NIGEL. Well, you can have the intelligent ones. Who have you got lined up for me?

LYDIA. For the first experiment I have chosen myself—and Corporal Forster. (*She rises and crosses to* R)

NIGEL. Sounds a pretty fair cross-section, I must say.

DAVID. We think so.

NIGEL. I hope you'll both be very happy. I know Eve and I shall. (*He moves to the door* L)

LYDIA. Not so fast. Before we arrive at a decision, there are one or two tests to make.

NIGEL (*moving* C) Tests? What sort of tests?

(CONSTANCE *and* MONICA *enter* L. *They are now made-up and dressed for dinner in expensive but old-fashioned evening gowns*)

CONSTANCE. Ah, Lydia! How's everything going?

LYDIA. I was just about to start the tests.

CONSTANCE. Ah, yes, the tests. I know you scientists set great store by them, but as a layman, I mistrust them.

NIGEL. Remind me to vote for you at the next election.

CONSTANCE. Thank you. My seat, however, is quite safe. (*She turns to Monica with a smile. Her back is to Nigel*)

NIGEL (*viewing Constance's back with displeasure*) That doesn't surprise me.

CONSTANCE (*turning*) I'm glad, because nothing you say or do would surprise me. I imagine I can tell the Minister all she wants to know without the aid of a test.

NIGEL (*sitting on the left arm of the sofa*) Go ahead.

CONSTANCE. Intelligence—limited. Manners—non-existent. Personality—unprepossessing. Immoral, conceited and rapacious in money matters.

NIGEL (*after a pause*) Nobody's perfect.

MONICA. But some are more so than others.

CONSTANCE. At least, we have Professor Moxton.

MONICA. Haven't we, Professor?

DAVID. Oh, have you? Yes, I suppose you have, in a way.

NIGEL. But he's not exactly an enthusiast.

DAVID (*rising*) Oh, but I am. (*He suddenly realizes the implication of his remark*) I mean—the unique scientific problem—(*he resumes his seat*) is—er—unique.

NIGEL (*rising*) Let's face it. I was born for this moment. It's Destiny.

MONICA. I never did care for Destiny.

NIGEL. Anyway, I haven't time to talk to you now. Lydia's having a look at my Id.

CONSTANCE. That is something I couldn't bear to witness. Come, Monica, let's dine.

(CONSTANCE *and* MONICA *exit* L)

NIGEL (*to Lydia*) Well, what are we waiting for? (*He moves* LC)

(LYDIA *moves* R *and presses the bell-push*)

LYDIA (*moving down* R) I was wondering whether it's worth wasting time on Corporal Forster. Her characteristics are obviously predictable—(*she refers to her notebook*) feather-brained, easy-going, and incredibly stupid. (*She crosses to* C)

NIGEL. No Id, but plenty of Bod.

LYDIA. I'll test you first, Professor.

DAVID (*rising*) You will? I say, this is quite exciting.

(DORA *enters* L)

DORA. You rang—(*she looks at Nigel*) I hope.

(NIGEL *retreats up* C)

LYDIA. You were quick.

DORA. You get a move on when you've something to live for. What do you want?

LYDIA. George.

DORA. He's asleep.

LYDIA. Wake him up, bring him here, and take Wing Commander Lawler for a walk.

NIGEL (*moving down* LC) What?

DORA. I don't need no dog to protect me.

LYDIA (*crossing to the door* L) No, I can see that. You can take the Colonel along, too. (*She opens the door and calls*) Colonel.

NIGEL. I don't want a walk.

DORA. Didn't you drink your tea, then?

NIGEL (*to Lydia*) Are you trying to get rid of me?

LYDIA. I require an atmosphere of sanity. With you in the room that would be inconceivable.

(*The* MAJOR *enters* L)

MAJOR (*saluting*) Colonel Danvers-Bishop reporting.

LYDIA. Take this man for a walk.

NIGEL. I protest.

MAJOR. With pleasure. (*She draws her gun*) Prisoner and escort—'shun!

(DORA *and* NIGEL *spring to attention*)

Left turn. Quick march. Left, right—left, right . . .

(NIGEL *and* DORA *march off* L.
*The* MAJOR *follows them off*. LYDIA *closes the door*)

DAVID. Poor Nigel. He hates exercise.

LYDIA. So I gather.

(*There is a pause*)

DAVID. I do, too.

LYDIA. Really?

(*There is a pause.* LYDIA *moves to* L *of the table* C)

DAVID (*rising*) Yes, well, I'm ready if you are.
LYDIA. Good.

(DAVID *moves to* R *of the table* C *and faces* LYDIA *across it*)

DAVID. You know, this I.Q. business is quite exciting. I'm most anxious to know whether the enforced mental atrophy of suspended animation has any detrimental intellectual effects. What do you think?
LYDIA. Just the opposite.
DAVID. Really? Why is that?
LYDIA. I believe that forced inactivity in—any direction causes a tremendous build-up.
DAVID. Do you? That's most interesting.
LYDIA. You'll probably issue forth intelligence like a burst dam, just as some people give vent to their—er—emotions—after a period of abstinence.
DAVID. I think not. No, I can't see that the analogy is a valid one. You see, in the first place . . .
LYDIA. Does it matter?
DAVID. I beg your pardon?
LYDIA. I'm not really going to test you, you know.
DAVID. Oh.
LYDIA. It was an excuse to get your friend out of the way.
DAVID. Oh.
LYDIA. You say "Oh" quite a lot, don't you?
DAVID (*moving above the table*) Do I? Yes, I suppose I do.
LYDIA (*moving to* L *of David*) Why?
DAVID. I don't know. I've never thought about it.
LYDIA. Probably because you're rather shy and easily embarrassed.
DAVID. That's probably it.
LYDIA. There's no need to be, you know. Not with me, at any rate.
DAVID. Thank you.
LYDIA. You see, we have so much in common.
DAVID. Rather! Both double firsts at Oxford.
LYDIA. I wasn't only thinking of that.
DAVID. No?
LYDIA. No. Don't you ever want—just now and again—to forget all about your work?
DAVID. Actually——
LYDIA. Yes?
DAVID. —no. Do you?
LYDIA. Actually——
DAVID. Yes?
LYDIA. —nearly always.
DAVID. Good heavens!
LYDIA. Surprised?
DAVID. Tremendously. I thought were were dedicated.
LYDIA. Not really. It's an act I put on when the Thing happened.
DAVID. Oh.

LYDIA. Will you do me a favour?
DAVID. What sort of a favour?
LYDIA. Take off your glasses.
DAVID (*hesitantly*) My what?
LYDIA. Glasses.
DAVID. Oh.
LYDIA. Please.
DAVID. All right. (*He turns his back and removes his glasses*) There!

(LYDIA *takes David's glasses and puts them on the table* C. *She then removes her own glasses and places them to face his*)

Well?
LYDIA. Would you like to sit down?
DAVID. Where?
LYDIA. On the sofa.
DAVID. Oh. (*He moves to the sofa and sits, at the right end of it*)
LYDIA (*sitting* L *of David on the sofa*) Thank you.

(*There is a pause then* LYDIA *suddenly seizes David and kisses him passionately*)

Say it.
DAVID. Say what?
LYDIA. "Oh!"
DAVID. But I only say "Oh!" when I'm embarrassed.
LYDIA. You darling. (*She embraces and kisses him*)

(NIGEL *enters* L)

NIGEL. What a fascinating test.

(LYDIA *breaks from David and rises*)

Does it really measure intelligence?
LYDIA (*rushing to the table to reclaim her glasses*) What have you come back for? (*She realizes that she has put on David's glasses, and myopically changes them then moves to the windows*)
NIGEL (*moving* LC) There must be something in the air of this place. George ran off with an alsatian.
DAVID. Well, go and help catch them.
NIGEL. If I didn't know you better, I'd suspect you wanted me out of the way.
DAVID. I do.
NIGEL. Well, well! That's the fastest growth of libido I've ever seen.
DAVID. Really?
NIGEL. From a split pea to a melon in five minutes flat.
DAVID. I admit I have just experienced a most interesting chemical reaction.
LYDIA (*disappointed*) Chemical reaction? (*She moves up* R *of the table* C)
DAVID. Bio-chemical, to be precise.

LYDIA. Is that all?

DAVID. What else? I'm grateful to you, of course, for acting as a catalyst.

LYDIA. I'm glad to hear it.

DAVID. But of course the reaction was bound to take place sooner or later.

LYDIA. With anyone?

DAVID. Of similar bio-chemical characteristics.

LYDIA. Oh. (*She turns her back on David in mortification*)

NIGEL (*moving down* L) I do believe you're a woman after all, Lydia.

DAVID. Of course she's not. She's a scientist.

LYDIA. Oh!

DAVID. I do wish you wouldn't keep saying "Oh"!

(LYDIA *bursts into tears and runs off* L)

(*He rises*) What on earth did she do that for?

NIGEL (*moving* C) Don't you know?

DAVID. No.

NIGEL. Well, you'd better put your glasses back on. (*He hands David his glasses*) She's niggled.

DAVID. Why?

NIGEL. You as good as said that all women are roughly equal.

DAVID. Is that bad?

NIGEL. You might just as well have said that they're all equally rough.

DAVID (*sitting in the easy chair* R) I'm afraid I'm right out of my depth.

NIGEL. But the water's lovely when you get used to it.

DAVID. Well, she needn't have got so upset. It's unthinkable for men in our position to contemplate permanent liaisons. We must behave like . . .

NIGEL. Sultans?

DAVID. I was going to say "research workers with detached and clinical outlooks".

(*There is a knock at the door* L)

NIGEL (*calling*) Come in.

(EVE *enters* L. *She carries an apple*)

EVE. Hello.

DAVID (*rising*) Hell-o! (*He moves towards Eve, appreciating for the first time that she is attractive*)

NIGEL (*wagging his finger at David*) Ah-ah! "Detached and clinical".

DAVID (*moving down* R) Er, of course.

NIGEL. Come and sit down, Eve dear. The sofa's already been warmed.

EVE (*crossing to the sofa*) Thank you. (*She sits on the sofa, at the right end of it*) The Minister told me to come in and wait.

NIGEL. I hope you won't have to wait long.
EVE. She said I had to do a test.
NIGEL. Did she say what sort of test?
EVE. High I.Q.
NIGEL (*looking puzzled*) I like you, too. Oh, I see.
EVE. I think she wants to find out if we've both got one.
NIGEL. I'm sure we have. (*He sits* L *of Eve on the sofa*) Comfy?
EVE. Ever so.
NIGEL (*moving closer to Eve; to David*) Go outside and look for George.
DAVID. For who?
NIGEL. The bulldog.
DAVID. Why?
NIGEL. Don't be an idiot!
DAVID. Oh, yes, I see. Of course. (*He crosses to the door* L) Quite. (*He opens the door*)

(LYDIA *enters* L. *She carries a stop-watch*)

(*He bumps into Lydia*) I'm so sorry. I was just going to see a dog about a man—I mean . . .
LYDIA. Some other time, Professor. I want you to assist me with the tests. (*She crosses to* L *of the sofa*)
DAVID (*moving* C) But you said . . .
LYDIA. On the Wing Commander and Corporal Forster. (*She hands the watch to David*) Wing Commander, stand over there. (*She motions Nigel to a position* RC) Corporal, you'll do nicely where you are.

(DAVID *moves* L)

NIGEL (*rising and moving* RC) We've been doing nicely for the past five minutes. And given a few more, we'd have shown you how compatible we were without a test. Isn't that so, Eve?
EVE. Yes. What's compatible?
NIGEL. Never mind.
LYDIA (*to David*) Over here, please.
DAVID (*moving* LC) All right, we're ready. Let's have the questions.
EVE. I'm not much good at answering questions.
NIGEL. You know how to say "yes", don't you?
EVE. Yes.
NIGEL. Then it's as easy as getting out of bed.
EVE. I don't find that at all easy.
NIGEL. Don't you?
LYDIA. Right, then, let us begin. I assume you've both heard of associations of words?
NIGEL. Yes.
EVE. No.
NIGEL. I mean—no.
LYDIA. I say a word, and you reply with the first word that comes into your head. Understand?
NIGEL. No.

EVE. Yes.

NIGEL. I mean—yes. See how compatible we are.

LYDIA. Right, I'll start with you, Corporal.

EVE. Isn't it exciting?

LYDIA. No.

EVE. Yes.

LYDIA. I mean, no, it isn't exciting. It isn't intended to be exciting.

EVE. Sorry.

LYDIA. All right.

EVE. O.K.

NIGEL. Sauce.

EVE. Bottle.

NIGEL. Milk.

EVE. Shake.

NIGEL. Shiver.

EVE. Twist.

NIGEL. Bust.

LYDIA. Stop! Stop! Stop!

EVE. Go! Go! Go!

(LYDIA *struggles to preserve her self-control*)

LYDIA. If you don't mind, we'll start again without your assistance, Wing Commander. (*To Eve*) Are you ready?

EVE. 'Course.

LYDIA. Mother.

EVE. Father.

LYDIA. Brother.

EVE. Sister.

LYDIA. Son.

EVE. Moon.

LYDIA. I meant S-O-N.

EVE. Sorry. Er—B-O-Y.

LYDIA. There is no need to spell your answer.

EVE. Why not? You spelled your question.

LYDIA (*sardonically*) Thank you.

EVE. Please.

LYDIA. Thank you—the test is over.

EVE. Pity. I was enjoying it.

LYDIA. I wasn't. Now, Wing Commander.

NIGEL. Ready, able and willing.

LYDIA. I hope so. Flower.

(EVE *crosses her legs*)

NIGEL. Bed. (*He gazes at Eve, admiring her legs*)

LYDIA. Wine.

NIGEL. Women.

LYDIA. Mother.

NIGEL. Love.

LYDIA. Middle.

NIGEL. Sex.
LYDIA. Cheese.
NIGEL. Cake.
LYDIA. Water.
NIGEL. Leg.
LYDIA. Fire.
NIGEL. Leg.
LYDIA. What on earth are you talking about?
NIGEL. Sorry—got diverted. Where were we?
LYDIA. At the end of a useless five minutes.
NIGEL. You mean—that's all?
LYDIA. It would be a waste of time to continue.
DAVID. I agree.
LYDIA. Your mental capacities are so similar and so remarkably shallow that even if we continued all night no further facts about them could possibly emerge.
NIGEL (*crossing to Lydia*) We're compatible?
LYDIA. Compatible? You're identical.
NIGEL. Just made for each other.
LYDIA. Under conditions of natural selectivity—yes.
NIGEL (*turning*) Eve! (*He holds out his arms*)

(EVE *rises*)

(*He moves to Eve and embraces her*) Give me a bite of that apple.
LYDIA. Just a minute. I haven't finished yet.
NIGEL. And I haven't started yet.
LYDIA. The nation is not interested in producing a generation of subnormal intellects.
NIGEL. Hard luck.
LYDIA. Thus, for natural selection we substitute . . .
DAVID. Scientific manipulation?
LYDIA. Exactly.
NIGEL (*releasing Eve and turning*) What?
LYDIA. Pairing by design, and not by choice. Brains with brawn.
DAVID. Beauty with intellect.
LYDIA. In other words—(*to Nigel*) you and I—Corporal Forster . . .
DAVID. And me?
LYDIA. Yes.
NIGEL. This is ridiculous.
LYDIA. It's fully in accordance with correct genetic principles.
NIGEL. I don't care what it's in accorance with. Eve and I won't stand for it. Will we, Eve?
EVE. Stand for what? (*She sits on the sofa*)
NIGEL (*to Eve*) Never mind. (*To Lydia*) You can't break us up like this.
LYDIA. The matter is settled.
NIGEL. Like hell it is. I'll go on strike.
LYDIA. You can't.
NIGEL. Who says?

LYDIA. It's illegal under the Nationalized Industries Act.
NIGEL. Then I'll go to prison.
LYDIA. Holloway?
DAVID. Don't get so excited, Nigel. Things aren't so bad.
NIGEL. Of course they aren't—for you. But just think of me. With sons who can quote Pythagoras between bottles.
DAVID. If they can, no-one will be more grateful than their mother.
NIGEL. She won't have the chance. If she as much as comes near me, I shall . . .
LYDIA. Scream?
NIGEL. Very likely.
LYDIA. Then let me set your mind at rest. I shall never be nearer to you than the length of a laboratory bench. (*She moves to* L *of the table* C)
NIGEL. Eh?
LYDIA. Science is seldom at a loss, as any veterinary surgeon will tell you. Cross-breeding in that field has long passed the experimental stage.
NIGEL. So I'm an Aberdeen Shorthorn now, am I?
LYDIA (*moving to the french windows*) Exactly.
NIGEL (*to David*) Did you hear that? Did you hear what she said?
DAVID. Yes.
NIGEL. You realize the implications?
DAVID. Of course. And I think it's an absolutely tremendous idea.
NIGEL. You're mad. Don't you agree, Eve?
EVE (*uncomprehending*) Me?
NIGEL. Never mind. (*To Lydia*) I've never heard of anything so inhuman—so diabolical—and as far as co-operation from me is concerned, you've had it. Completely and utterly. So you can get that idea right out of your Right Honourable nut.

(NIGEL *exits* R, *slamming the door behind him*)

EVE (*rising*) Well! Someone got out of bed the wrong side this morning, didn't they? (*She moves to the door* R)
LYDIA (*moving quickly and intercepting Eve*) Where are you going?
EVE. To guard him, of course.
LYDIA (*leading Eve to the door* L) Do it from the garden, dear.

(LYDIA *pushes* EVE *out* L)

We mustn't encourage any more bio-chemical reactions, must we, Professor?
DAVID (*miserably*) No—I suppose not.
LYDIA. I'm glad you agree.
DAVID. Although upon reflection I'm not convinced that the reaction we experienced was wholly chemical.
LYDIA (*coolly*) Really?
DAVID. Unless, of course, it was a chain reaction which is still continuing. That would explain it.

LYDIA. Explain what?

DAVID. The feeling I'm still getting.

LYDIA. Cold feet?

DAVID. No—no, quite the reverse. A perceptible rise in temperature whenever you come near me.

LYDIA. How interesting.

DAVID. Oh, it is. In fact, I've noticed it before—with frogs.

LYDIA. Under experimental conditions.

DAVID. Naturally. Although the experiments were inconclusive.

LYDIA. Perhaps you should try some more.

DAVID. Oh, I will. (*He moves* C) But right now the only thing I can think of is . . . (*He hesitates*)

LYDIA. Yes.

DAVID. Trying our experiment all over again.

(LYDIA *makes a slight move* RC *towards David.*
CONSTANCE *and* MONICA *enter* L, *dressed in cycling outfits*)

CONSTANCE. We are just off to the House.

LYDIA. Already? The debate isn't until tomorrow.

CONSTANCE. We're cycling.

LYDIA. Surely you don't need *more* exercise.

MONICA. We don't.

CONSTANCE. Speak for yourself, Monica.

MONICA. I did.

CONSTANCE (*crossing to* R) Where is the Wing Commander?

LYDIA. In bed with a sore head, I think.

CONSTANCE (*sitting on the sofa*) The tests were too much for him, eh?

LYDIA. Probably. Look, if your car's out of order . . .

CONSTANCE. It isn't. Our mode of travel is a political expedient.

MONICA (*moving* LC) Marchbanks plans to split the Cabinet.

CONSTANCE. So I shall retaliate by pointing out that nobody can take seriously the opinions of a Minister who travels round the country reviewing non-existent fleets.

MONICA. By Rolls Royce

CONSTANCE. Chauffeur-driven.

MONICA. When the nation is suffering from a grave petrol shortage.

LYDIA. That should stop her.

MONICA. Almost.

CONSTANCE. The *piece de resistance* will be when I casually remove my cycle clips.

LYDIA. Brilliant!

CONSTANCE. And calmly announce that I have assured the continuance of the human race. (*She rises triumphantly*)

MONICA. We shall arrive back tomorrow evening.

CONSTANCE. By Rolls Royce.

MONICA. Chauffeur-driven.

DAVID. But you're not going to tell them about—us?

CONSTANCE. Certainly.

DAVID. Can't it wait?
CONSTANCE. No.
MONICA. We are going to use you . . .
CONSTANCE. To remain in office.
MONICA. Time to go, P.M. (*She moves to the door* L *and holds it open*)
CONSTANCE. So it is. Wish me luck, Lydia.
LYDIA. I'll see you off, but you won't need luck.
CONSTANCE (*crossing to* L) No, I don't think I will. With my men I'll be safe for another twenty years.

(CONSTANCE, LYDIA *and* MONICA *exit* L. DAVID *crosses to* R. NIGEL *bursts in excitedly* R)

NIGEL. I've got it!
DAVID. What?
NIGEL. The answer. Where's Lydia?
DAVID. Seeing the Prime Minister off.
NIGEL. Good. We've no time to lose.
DAVID. What are you talking about?
NIGEL. You and I are going to escape.
DAVID. Us?
NIGEL. See to those alarms and booby traps.
DAVID. No.
NIGEL. Why not?
DAVID (*moving* L) I'm not going to escape.
NIGEL (*following David and catching him by the arm*) There are twenty-six million women out there.
DAVID. Well?
NIGEL. I can only cope with half of them.
DAVID. I don't care.
NIGEL. Then start caring, because when I get out, do you know what I'm going to do?
DAVID. What?
NIGEL (*pointing towards the window*) I'm going to tell them out there—that you are in here. (*He pokes David in the chest*)
DAVID. You wouldn't.
NIGEL. I would. (*He moves to* R *of the window*) And they'll mob the place.
DAVID (*moving to* L *of Nigel*) This is blackmail.
NIGEL. You catch on quick. Coming?
DAVID. I've no choice.
NIGEL. Good. Now for those gadgets.
DAVID. What about the dogs?
NIGEL. Lord, yes. (*He moves down* R, *thinking furiously*)
DAVID. They attack anything in trousers.
NIGEL. Then we won't wear any.
DAVID (*horrified*) I couldn't go out there in my underpants.
NIGEL. We'll get hold of a couple of skirts.
DAVID. That won't fool them.
NIGEL. They won't know the difference. Not from the women round here.

David. Dogs rely on scent.

Nigel (*turning to David*) That's it. Scent. We'll soak ourselves in scent.

(Dora *enters* L, *carrying a tray with two cups of tea*)

Dora, not again!

Dora. Then I'll give it to George.

Nigel. He's back?

Dora. The alsatian and him didn't hit it off.

Nigel (*moving* C) So much for cross-breeding.

Dora. This'll go with his biscuit. Colonel Bogie's just giving him one.

Nigel. Only one?

Dora. She's keeping him hungry.

Nigel. I see. (*He suddenly has an idea*) I—er—wish she'd keep him sweet as well.

Dora. Sweet?

Nigel. He pongs. When he deposits his bulk outside that door it's like Battersea Dogs' Home in August.

Dora. I can't help it.

Nigel. How about a few drops of strong perfume to sprinkle around?

Dora. I've got a bottle upstairs.

Nigel. *Have* you?

Dora. I'll get it.

Nigel. Angel! (*He takes the tray from Dora*)

Dora. But with both feet on the ground. After all, a girl don't buy a perfume called "Original Sin" for nothing.

(Dora *exits* L)

Nigel (*putting the tray on the table* C) See? Now for the skirts.

David. Whose?

Nigel. Eve's and Dora's.

David. But how?

Nigel (*moving to David*) We make love to them.

David. That's unthinkable.

Nigel. I tell you what I'll do, as I'm a sportsman. You can have Dora.

David. Thank you.

Nigel. Don't mention it.

David. But I wouldn't know what to say.

Nigel. Then I'll go first.

David. With Dora?

Nigel. No—Eve. (*He leads David down* R) You can go in there and listen through the keyhole.

David. I am not a Peeping Tom.

Nigel. I'm not asking you to peep—just listen.

David. I don't like it. Suppose I can't hear you?

Nigel. Knock three times and I'll speak up.

(EVE *enters* L)

Ah, Eve, come in. You'll have to excuse the Professor. (*He moves* C) He's just going to lie down.

DAVID. To what?

NIGEL. To lie down. (*He indicates the door* R) Through there.

DAVID. What for?

NIGEL. To get rid of that headache.

DAVID. Headache? Oh, yes, of course.

(DAVID *exits* R)

NIGEL. Come and sit down on the sofa.

EVE (*crossing to the sofa*) Oh, I can't do that. I'm on guard.

NIGEL. I'll just sit on the arm, then you needn't be—on guard. (*He sits on the left arm of the sofa*)

(EVE *sits on the sofa*)

Comfy?

EVE. Yes, thanks.

NIGEL. I suppose this is the first time you've been alone with a man since the night before the Calamity?

EVE. I wasn't with one that night.

NIGEL. What a terrible waste.

EVE. I was on duty.

NIGEL. Doing what?

EVE. Now let me think—I was . . .

NIGEL. On guard?

EVE. How did you guess?

(NIGEL *slides off the sofa arm, sits* L *of Eve on the sofa and puts his arm around her. There are three loud knocks on the door* R)

NIGEL (*loudly*) What do you do in the Army?

EVE. Security and all that.

NIGEL (*loudly*) And before you joined?

EVE. I drove a tractor for me dad.

NIGEL. That's why they put you in an ambulance?

EVE. I suppose so.

NIGEL. I've never been in an ambulance.

EVE. You have. I drove you down in one.

NIGEL. I meant—as a casualty.

EVE. I've never been on my back in one, either.

NIGEL. I should hope not. I mean, I can't imagine those lovely features or that perfect figure being marred by an accident.

EVE. Nor can I.

NIGEL. That test was fascinating. Fancy us being so alike. And you such a beautiful girl.

EVE. Do you think this uniform suits me?

NIGEL. I'd like to see you without it—I mean, in something else.

EVE. I haven't got anything else.

NIGEL. Not even—a greatcoat?

Eve. Oh, yes.

Nigel. I'd like to see you in your greatcoat.

Eve. You're a funny bloke, you are. Most men I've known tried to make me take things off, not put 'em on.

Nigel. I'm different.

Eve (*suspiciously*) Oh?

Nigel (*hastily*) That is—well, I'm a man for all that, if you know what I mean.

Eve. I like my men—rugged.

Nigel. Rugged? My dear girl, I'm corrugated.

Eve. Are you?

Nigel. And seething with manly vigour.

(*They kiss. There are three knocks on the door* R.
Dora *enters* R, *carrying a bottle of scent. As she sees* Nigel *and* Eve *kissing, she crosses to the table* C *and slams the bottle down on it*)

Dora. Your scent!

(Dora *exits* L)

Eve (*rising*) Scent? (*She seems shocked*)

Nigel (*rising*) Oh, it's not for me. (*He goes to the table* C *and sniffs the scent*)

Eve. No?

Nigel. No, it's for David. You see . . . Oh, I suppose I'll have to tell you. (*He moves to Eve*) David and I are going to escape.

Eve. Escape?

Nigel. Disguised in your clothes and smothered in scent. To fool the dogs.

Eve. You'll never do it.

Nigel. We can—with your help. Will you help us?

Eve. Only if . . . (*She hesitates*)

Nigel. Yes?

Eve. If you take me with you.

Nigel. It's a deal. (*He kisses her*) Get the greatcoat. (*He pushes Eve to the door* L)

(Eve *exits* L)

(*He moves* C *and calls*) David. You can come out.

(David *enters* R)

Well? Did you learn anything? (*He crosses to* R *and presses the bell-push*)

David. I don't know. I've never heard anything like it before.

Nigel (*crossing to* LC) And I hope you never will again. I'm badly out of practice.

David. I've never practised at all.

Nigel (*crossing to David*) Now's your chance to try. Don't worry. Dora's a pushover.

David. I'd far rather you administered the push.

Nigel. Be fair. I've done my bit.

DAVID. Couldn't you do another bit?

(DORA *enters* L)

DORA (*to Nigel; coldly*) You wanted me?
NIGEL. No—he did.
DAVID (*in a panic*) I?
NIGEL. He'd like a word with you.

(NIGEL *exits* R)

DORA. Well?
DAVID. Er—come and sit down on the sofa.
DORA (*crossing to the sofa*) Sure. (*She sits on the sofa*) Anything to oblige.
DAVID I—I . . .
DORA. Aren't you going to sit down?
DAVID. Thank you. (*He sits on the sofa, as far away from Dora as possible*)
DORA. Comfy?
DAVID. You shouldn't say that. I say it. I mean . . .
DORA. Well?
DAVID. Perhaps I ought to sit on your arm.
DORA. On my what?
DAVID. Arm. Then I needn't be on my guard.
DORA. Is something worrying you?
DAVID. Yes—no. I mean . . . This is the first time I've been alone with a woman since the night before the Calamity.
DORA. Oh, you poor boy. (*She moves sympathetically towards him*)
DAVID. Er, what did you do in the Army?
DORA. The Army? I've never been in the Army.
DAVID. No, of course not. You drove a tractor for your dad.
DORA. Are you feeling all right?
DAVID. Oh, yes, I'm in excellent health. I've never been in an ambulance.
DORA. Haven't you now?
DAVID. No. I can't imagine my face and body ever being marred by an accident.
DORA. I can, at the rate you're going on. 'Ere, you have got something to say to me?
DAVID. Oh, yes.
DORA. Well, you're a queer one, I must say.
DAVID. Oh, no, I'm not. I'm seething with manly vigour.
DORA. Yes. I can hear you.
DAVID. And I'm certainly rugged enough.
DORA. I'm glad to hear it.
DAVID. So am I.

(*There is a pause*)

DORA. Shall I fetch you a book?
DAVID. Yes—I mean—no, thank you.
DORA. Well, what is it?

DAVID. I can't remember.

(*Three knocks are heard at the door* R)

(*He remembers*) Perhaps if I kissed you, it would come back to me.

DORA. Kissed me?

DAVID. If you wouldn't mind.

DORA. Mind? What are we waiting for? (*She pounces on David and vigorously kisses him*) There! Has that helped you remember?

DAVID (*gasping*) Yes.

DORA. Then there was something else you wanted?

DAVID. Yes.

DORA. What?

DAVID. It's rather delicate.

DORA. Go on.

DAVID. Would you mind letting me have your skirt?

DORA. My skirt?

DAVID. Please.

DORA. 'Ere. Is this some new technique for getting me clothes off?

DAVID. Good gracious me! What a shocking idea.

DORA (*puzzled*) You *don't* want me to take my clothes off?

DAVID. Most certainly not. Any you have lying around will suit me equally well.

DORA. 'Ere! If you carry on like this I'll start to think it's me clothes and not me you're interested in.

DAVID. But it is—I mean—I like you, naturally, but at the moment I'd like to see your skirt without you in it.

DORA (*rising*) 'Ave you gone barmy?

DAVID. I only want to wear it for a little while, and I couldn't with you in it, now could I?

(EVE *enters* L, *carrying her greatcoat.* DAVID *rises and moves down* R)

DORA (*crossing to Eve*) Thank God you've come. I've got a right one here, I can tell you.

EVE. Sorry. Can't stop. Where's Nigel?

DORA (*indicating the door* R) Through there.

(EVE *crosses to the door* R)

EVE (*as she opens the door*) I've brought your . . .

(NIGEL *falls into the room*)

What on earth are you doing?

NIGEL. Just dropping in.

EVE. Well, get up. (*She holds up the coat*) And get this on.

NIGEL. Well done.

(EVE *helps* NIGEL *to put on the coat*)

DORA. What *is* this?

NIGEL. Nothing, Dora. You can carry on buttling. (*He rolls up his trousers legs*)

DORA. Blimey, another one!
NIGEL. How's that for a spot of *Folies Bergere?*
EVE. Revolting!
NIGEL. Nonsense, they're every bit as good as the Major's.
DORA. I'm getting out of this. (*She darts towards the door* L)

(NIGEL *moves quickly and intercepts Dora*)

NIGEL. No, you don't.
DORA. Let me go.
NIGEL. Not till we've escaped.
DORA. Escaped?
NIGEL. That's why I'm dressing up. The dogs attack anything in pants, remember?
DORA. You mean—you're gonna leave here?
NIGEL. 'Fraid so. (*He leads Dora* C)
DORA. What about me?
NIGEL. You? Oh, you're coming with us, naturally.
DORA. And her?
NIGEL. Eve, too.
DORA. Is that why 'e wanted that skirt?
NIGEL. That's it. Got one?
DORA. Only this.
DAVID. That settles it. I'll have to stay behind (*He moves towards the door* R)
DORA (*quickly intercepting David*) What about a blanket? Wrapped round his middle.
NIGEL. Dora, you're a genius.
EVE. There's some in there.

(DORA *exits* R)

NIGEL. I protest.
EVE. Don't forget the Colonel, will you?
NIGEL. Shall I ever?
EVE (*moving to the window*) She's in her room, watching the terrace.
NIGEL. With a gun?
EVE. Yes.
DAVID (*moving to Nigel*) As soon as those alarms go off she'll start shooting.
NIGEL. She's probably crouched over her backsight at this very minute.
EVE (*moving between Nigel and David*) You could cut the lead.
NIGEL. How?
EVE. Break a window. It runs up the wall outside.
NIGEL. That's it.

(DORA *enters* R *carrying a tartan rug*)

DORA. 'Ere we are. Mind you, it ain't a Christian Dior.
NIGEL. It's more like a Sandy MacTavish. David! Strip!
DAVID. What?

NIGEL. Remove your trousers.

(DORA *crosses and gives the rug to David*)

DAVID. I'll do nothing of the sort.
NIGEL (*moving to David*) This is no time for modesty.
DAVID. Keep away! I'll shout for the Colonel.
NIGEL. Spare his blushes, girls. Nip into the bedroom.
DORA. We won't look.

(DORA *and* EVE *turn away up* R *of the sofa and cover their eyes*)

DAVID. Yes, but you might hear.
DORA. Oh, orl right. Come on, Eve. You can tell he wasn't in the Boy Scouts.

(DORA *exits* R)

EVE. Don't be long. I can't wait to get to Gretna Green.

(EVE *exits* R)

NIGEL. Gretna Green? Did you hear that?
DAVID. Draw the curtains, please.
NIGEL. For crying out loud! Come here. (*He wraps the rug around David and knots it into position*) If you think anyone's going to write to *The Times* saying, "Today I saw my first underpants . . ." Now slide your trousers off.
DAVID. This is most undignified.
NIGEL. Now, here's the drill. You break the window and cut the wire as soon as I give the word. (*He goes to the door* R *and quietly turns the key*)
DAVID. What are you doing?
NIGEL. Shush! I'm locking them in.
DAVID. But they're coming with us.
NIGEL. There's no point in carrying coals to Newcastle.
DAVID. This is despicable.
NIGEL. Not with Gretna Green as their first objective. Get those trousers off. You look ridiculous.

(DAVID *steps out of his trousers*)

DAVID. We are double-crossing our allies.
NIGEL. Get this straight. When we get out there we won't find a world full of allies. Every woman under seventy is a potential enemy. Now, we make a racket—the Colonel will try to come in here. We barricade the door—and away.
DORA (*off*) Can we come in now? (*She rattles the door*)
NIGEL. We're rumbled.
DORA (*off*) Hey, what's the idea?

(EVE *and* DORA, *off, start to yell in unison*)

NIGEL. She'll have the Colonel in.
DAVID. Isn't that what what we want?

NIGEL. Not yet. We're not ready. I know. (*He moves to the record-player and switches it on*) Now, get that scent on.

(*A Highland reel blares from the record-player.*

LYDIA *enters* L. NIGEL *seizes* DAVID *and forces him to join him in a Highland fling. Between them, they whirl* LYDIA *round and out of the door* L)

Quick!

(DAVID *pushes the sofa against the door* L. NIGEL *breaks the window with a vase.* DAVID *goes to the window and pulls in what appears to be a length of cable*)

Give it a jerk.

(DAVID *jerks the wire, which comes into the room covered with roots*)

Fool! That's a creeper. (*He forces the windows open*)

(*The alarm rings.* DAVID *and* NIGEL *sprinkle themselves with scent*)

Now!

*The door* L *bursts open, forcing the sofa aside.*

*The* MAJOR *staggers into the room.* DAVID *and* NIGEL *rush out by the french windows. The* MAJOR *fires a shot.* DAVID *loses his blanket. As they go through the window a net descends on them.*

CURTAIN

Blackout

# ACT III

SCENE—*The same. The following afternoon.*

*When the* CURTAIN *rises,* NIGEL *is standing above the sofa, so the audience do not yet see there is a ball and chain attached to his leg. He is smoking moodily.* DAVID *is sitting on the sofa, reading a book. Outside the window, up a step-ladder, the legs of the* MAJOR *are just visible and she can be heard hammering. The hammering reaches a crescendo then stops abruptly. There is a pause.*

NIGEL. Have you noticed something?

DAVID. Yes, the hammering's stopped.

NIGEL. No, I meant we're back to square one. Only this time it's worse.

DAVID. Why?

NIGEL. The Major's up the ladder.

DAVID. So that's why your nose isn't pressed to the glass.

NIGEL. God, what a day it's been. I almost wish the old P.M. was back.

DAVID (*shocked*) You haven't got designs on her.

NIGEL. Don't be an idiot!

DAVID. It wouldn't surprise me in the least. After seeing you operate I wouldn't trust you with my grandmother. And she's been dead for five years.

NIGEL. Here she comes.

(*The* MAJOR *descends the ladder*)

I suppose dry rot in the steps is too much to hope for.

(*The* MAJOR *glowers in at* NIGEL *who smiles and waves to her.* NIGEL *then turns and pulls a face registering repulsion. When he turns back to the window the* MAJOR *is still glowering in at him.* NIGEL *forces a smile and waves to her.*

*The* MAJOR *exits outside the window to* L)

I say!

DAVID. What's the matter, now?

NIGEL. A ghastly thought's just occurred to me.

DAVID. What?

NIGEL. Do you think I could ever get desperate enough to fancy the Major?

DAVID. Do you mind? I'm trying to read. If you want to turn over your subconscious compost heap do it quietly.

(NIGEL *moves to the table* C, *revealing the ball and chain. He lights a fresh cigarette*)

NIGEL. Smoking is the only vice I have left.

DAVID. You mean the only one you can indulge in at the moment.
NIGEL. You try indulging in vice with your leg manacled. (*He picks up the ball*)
DAVID. You cannot manacle a leg. You can only manacle a hand.
NIGEL. That consoles me no end. What are you reading? (*He sits* L *of David on the sofa and puts the ball on the seat beside him*)
DAVID. Nothing.
NIGEL. Molecular theory?
DAVID. No.
NIGEL. Calculus?
DAVID. No.
NIGEL. What, then?
DAVID. *Fanny Hill.*
NIGEL. Good heavens! Far too advanced.
DAVID. Why?
NIGEL. You should start on something much more elementary.
DAVID. Such as . . . ?
NIGEL. *Tom Jones.*
DAVID. Actually I'm only reading it in self-defence.
NIGEL. Why's that?
DAVID. So I've some idea of what everyone keeps talking about.
NIGEL. Well, mind you don't become too expert, or they'll legacle you, too.

(*The* MAJOR *enters* L *and stands to one side*)

MAJOR. Room—shun!

(DAVID *and* NIGEL *rise.*
CONSTANCE, MONICA *and* LYDIA *enter* L. CONSTANCE *moves* C. MONICA *remains by the door* L. LYDIA *moves to the window*)

NIGEL. Here comes trouble.
CONSTANCE. Well, I've done it.
NIGEL. Congratulations.
CONSTANCE. The battle's won.
MONICA. Hands down.
CONSTANCE. I said I'd do it, and I did.
MONICA. You did indeed, P.M.
DAVID. What did you do?
CONSTANCE. I steered the Ship of State between the Scylla of Doubt and the Charybdis of Anarchy into the Open Waters of an Assured Future.
MONICA. I was navigating.
NIGEL. So you've announced our existence? (*He sits on the sofa*)
CONSTANCE. To a crowded House. It was an historic moment. You could have heard a pin drop. Then, when they realized the implications, uproar. The Speaker calling for order, and Marchbanks shouting . . .
MONICA (*shouting*) "If the Prime Minister has two men, where are they?"

Constance. Only louder.

David. I trust you didn't tell them. (*He sits in the easy chair* R)

Constance. Of course not. I said you were both in the Tower and within seconds a horde of five hundred M.P.s were charging along the Embankment.

Monica. The first time anyone has tried to break *in* to the Tower.

Nigel. They got in?

Monica. We don't know. We retired in the confusion.

Constance. You noticed Marchbanks' face?

Monica. I didn't like it.

Constance. I *loved* it.

Monica. Prime Minister, it is not possible to love that face.

Constance. She was utterly deflated.

Monica. I wish I could agree. To me she looked smug and self-satisfied.

Constance. What about?

Monica. I don't know.

Constance. These Service people are all the same. A decorative exterior with nothing inside.

Nigel. Thank you. (*He rises*)

Constance. We've been discussing your official status.

Nigel. Have we one?

Constance. We couldn't decide whether you come under the Home Office . . .

Monica. Or the Minister of Agriculture.

Constance (*seeing Nigel's ball and chain for the first time*) What's this?

Nigel. Part of my decorative exterior.

Major. My idea, P.M.

Lydia. We had trouble last night. An attempted escape.

Constance. Was there really? Well, he won't be able to escape where he's going, will he, Monica?

Monica. I think not, P.M.

Constance. Do you know where we're sending you?

Monica. To a nice, healthy little farm.

Constance. In the Outer Hebrides.

(Constance *crosses and exits* L.
Monica *and* Lydia *follow her off*)

Nigel (*moving* L) Wait! You can't.

(*The door is slammed in Nigel's face*)

If I get this off it'll go straight up her jumper.

Major. Now then, Wing Commander, watch your step.

Nigel (*moving to the sofa*) I can't do much else—with this on.

Major. I trust it's a snug fit.

Nigel. Fine.

Major. I bet you'd like to know where the key is.

Nigel. Down your flipping neck, I expect.
Major. Wrong. It's round George's. Tied to his collar.

(*The* Major *exits* L)

Nigel. When we divide them up, David, she's one of yours. (*He sits on the sofa and takes out his lighter*) I'll give 'em Outer Hebrides.
David. Personally, I consider it an excellent choice. Quiet, peaceful, conducive to study.

(Nigel *flicks on his lighter and starts to burn at his chain*)

Don't you know the melting point of iron?
Nigel. No.
David. One thousand five hundred and thirty-three degrees.
Nigel. Really? (*He continues with his lighter*)
David. Centigrade.
Nigel. Oh. (*He puts away the lighter*)
David. Surely you're not still scheming?
Nigel (*rising*) More than ever. (*He limps to the Reviving Kit on the table up* L)
David. Then you're on your own.
Nigel. Suits me.
David. You'll never get past the dogs with that on.
Nigel. I'm not going past the dogs, I'm going out the front door.
David. But the Major!
Nigel. How much of this jollop did they use to put you out? (*He takes out a bottle and the syringe*)
David. Four c.c.s
Nigel. H'm! (*He starts to fill the syringe*)
David (*rising*) What are you doing? (*He puts his book on the table* C *and crosses to Nigel*)
Nigel. Four c.c.s.
David. Look, if you're planning to get out of here unconscious . . .
Nigel. I'm not. This is for the Major.
David. You're mad. You'll never get within a foot of her.
Nigel. We'll see. (*He surveys the syringe cryptically*) As it's the old viper herself we'd better add one for the pot. (*He draws more fluid into the syringe*)
David. Nigel, I forbid it! You can get ten years for doping a woman.
Nigel. You're thinking of horses. (*He gives David a withering look, then turns to the trolley where there are the remains of breakfast, picks up an uneaten sausage and injects some fluid into it*)
David (*moving* R) You'll never get her to eat cold sausage.
Nigel. This is for George. (*He replaces the sausage*) For the Major, I've planned a more horrible fate. (*He moves to the sofa and places the syringe, point upwards, in the centre between two cushions*)
David. And exactly how do you intend to get her to sit on that?

NIGEL. I shall just say, "Put your artery on that."

(DORA *enters* L, *carrying a cup of tea. She looks darkly at Nigel, crosses and smilingly hands the cup of tea to David*)

DORA. For you. (*She simpers*)
DAVID. Thanks.
NIGEL. Don't I get one?
DORA (*to David*) Please inform this gentleman that him and me are not on speaking terms.
NIGEL. Look, about last night . . .
DORA (*to David*) And tell him to belt up.
DAVID. Er—Nigel . . .
NIGEL. I heard. Tell her I'd be obliged if she'll ask General Kitchener to pop in here for a moment.
DORA (*to David*) Ask him what for.
NIGEL. I've a point I'd like to bring to her attention.

(DAVID *picks up his book and sits carefully on the sofa, at the right end of it*)

DORA. I'll tell her when I'm ready. (*She moves to* L *of the sofa*) Right now I intend to talk to my friend here.
NIGEL. I'd wait till he's finished *Fanny Hill.*
DORA. Why?
NIGEL. Then you'll have something to talk about.
DORA (*moving to* L *of David*) I'll talk to him now. (*She starts to sit on the syringe*)
NIGEL (*moving quickly to Dora*) No! (*He grabs hold of Dora to prevent her sitting*)
DORA. 'Ere! What you doing?
NIGEL (*frantically*) I love you. It's torture to see you sitting by my rival. For God's sake have pity. And get away from that sofa.
DORA (*alarmed*) You've gone bonkers!
NIGEL. Stone bonkers. About you.
DORA (*crossing to* L) I think I'd better go for the Colonel.

(DORA *exits* L)

NIGEL. Phew! That was a near one. She nearly sat down.
DAVID. You won't find it so easy with the Major. Personally, I don't think she ever sits down.
NIGEL. Well, hardly ever.

(*The* MAJOR *enters* L)

Ah, General.
MAJOR. Colonel.
NIGEL. Colonel, General—it's all the same to me. Come in.
MAJOR. I am in.
NIGEL. So you are.
MAJOR. You wanted me?
NIGEL. Only in a metaphorical sense. Come and sit down.

MAJOR (*suspiciously*) Sit down?

NIGEL. Over here. On the sofa. (*He sits on the sofa at the left end of it*) A rose between two thorns. (*He indicates the space between David and himself*) Nice and comfy.

MAJOR (*crossing to* C) What's the game?

NIGEL. Game?

MAJOR. I'm on my guard, Wing Commander. You'll not catch me out again.

NIGEL. Oh, come. The past is over. I'm your prisoner. Vanquished in fair fight. Let's sit down and talk things over like brother officers. I mean sister officers.

MAJOR. Very well.

(NIGEL *turns and gives David a broad wink*)

(*She crosses and sits in the easy chair* R) Well, Wing Commander, I'm sitting.

NIGEL. What? No, not there. I meant over here.

MAJOR. There's no point in my sitting over there.

NIGEL. That's what you think.

MAJOR. I beg your pardon?

NIGEL. I mean it's more comfortable over here.

MAJOR. I'm quite comfortable where I am.

NIGEL. I can't chat with you over there.

MAJOR. You can if you speak up.

(NIGEL *rises and crosses to the Major, carrying the ball in his hand*)

NIGEL. What I wanted to say is most confidential. (*He sits on the arm of her chair*)

MAJOR (*scrambling to her feet*) Now then. Keep your distance.

NIGEL. General! No more suspicions, surely?

MAJOR. I don't trust you with that thing in your hands.

NIGEL. What—this? (*He throws the ball a few inches into the air, and catches it*)

MAJOR. Yes, that.

(NIGEL *steps towards the* MAJOR, *who backs away*)

NIGEL. You could relieve me of it.

MAJOR (*backing towards the sofa*) I warn you, I shall take steps.

NIGEL. About four, if you don't mind. (*He continues to advance*)

MAJOR. That's far enough. I warn you. (*She is now in front of the centre of the sofa*)

(NIGEL *takes another step*)

(*She draws her gun*) Hands up!

(NIGEL *puts his hands and drops the ball on to the* MAJOR's *foot. She howls and, clutching her foot, flops on to the sofa.* DAVID *rises*)

NIGEL. Bang on target! Now for George. (*He takes the sausage to the door* L, *opens the door and throws the sausage off* L)

(*There is a growl and a yelp, followed by silence.* NIGEL *closes the door and crosses to the sofa. The* MAJOR *sits in a trance*)

Isn't she out, yet?

(DAVID *shakes his head*)

Feeling O.K., now?

(*The* MAJOR *stops clutching her foot and leans back on the sofa, a look of contentment creeping across her face*)

That's it, old girl. You pop off to sleep for a few years.

MAJOR. Sleep? (*She opens her eyes and sits up*) Why? I feel marvellous.

NIGEL. You what?

MAJOR. Fit as a fiddle and twice as ferocious.

NIGEL. Oh, good Lord!

MAJOR. What's more—the pain's gone.

NIGEL. Both of them?

MAJOR. I feel smashing. (*She leans towards Nigel and winks*) If you know what I mean—Nige.

DAVID. The wrong bottle.

NIGEL. Oh, no!

MAJOR. What bottle?

NIGEL. Nothing.

MAJOR. Have you got a tiny snifter tucked away for old Arrie?

NIGEL. Who?

MAJOR. Arrie.

NIGEL. Who's Harry?

MAJOR. Little old me. Short for Araminta. (*She rises*) Let's have a ball. (*She waltzes round to the record-player and puts on a record*)

NIGEL. David, do something.

DAVID. It's your fault—you do something.

NIGEL. I haven't a clue.

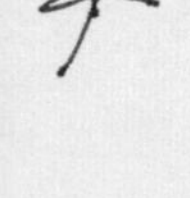

MAJOR. Live it up a bit. (*She switches on the record-player*) Do you know I haven't been to a dance since V.J. Day?

NIGEL. She wants us to dance.

MAJOR. La-de-dah-de-dah, bom-bomp! (*She hums and dances in tune to the music, a Saint Bernard's Waltz*)

NIGEL. Try the Professor.

MAJOR. What's wrong with you?

NIGEL. Slight handicap. (*He indicates his ball and chain*)

(*The* MAJOR *grabs* DAVID *and forces him into a stilted Saint Bernard's Waltz.* NIGEL *moves to the door* R *and holds it open. He then collects David's book and as* DAVID *exits with the* MAJOR, *dancing through the door* R, NIGEL *gives the book to David.* NIGEL *then crosses to the record-player and switches it off, just before the two loud beats. From off* R, *in synchronization, comes the sound of two loud thuds.*

DAVID *enters* R, *carrying his book and the Major's gun*)

DAVID. I've just proved that a man of intellect can also be a man of action.

NIGEL. You clocked her?
DAVID. With *Fanny Hill*.
NIGEL. Congratulations!
DAVID. What now?
NIGEL. We beat it.

(DAVID *and* NIGEL *cross to the door* L)

I'll take that. (*He takes the Major's gun*) I'm feeling murderous.

(DORA *and* EVE *enter* L)

DORA. Just where do you think you're going?
NIGEL. Nowhere.
DORA. So you're trying it on again.
NIGEL. What?
DORA. Escaping.
NIGEL. We wouldn't escape without taking you two along.
DORA. Like last night?
NIGEL. I can explain that.
DORA. Locking us in?
NIGEL. It was David.
EVE. David?
NIGEL. He refused to take off his trousers until the door was locked.
DAVID. I most certainly did . . .

(NIGEL *kicks David's shin*)

Oh! (*He crosses to the easy chair* R, *sits and nurses his shin*)
EVE. There! I said we weren't being fair on him.
NIGEL. You're forgiven. Now let's all get out of here. Get that key from George.
DORA. I can't.
NIGEL. Don't play games, Dora.
DORA. He's gone barmy. Chased the alsatians out the front gate.
NIGEL. What! I give up. I absolutely and utterly give up. Fate's against me, and you can't buck Fate. (*He moves to the sofa and sits, completely deflated*)

(CONSTANCE, MONICA *and* LYDIA *enter* L. LYDIA *moves to the window*)

CONSTANCE. What are you doing here?
DORA. We're—er . . .
CONSTANCE (*crossing to the table* C) Fraternizing?
DORA. No. Keeping an eye on them.
CONSTANCE. That's the Colonel's job. Where is she?
DAVID. Out.
NIGEL. With the dogs.
DAVID. For a walk.
CONSTANCE. Dora. Corporal. Find her. Both of you. Quick.

(DORA *and* EVE *exit* L)

Now about last night. What made you do it?

(*There is no reply*)

Aren't you happy here?

NIGEL. What do you think?

CONSTANCE. Oh, come, don't be downhearted. We'll treat you well—within reason. And when your work is done I shall be able to repeat those famous words, "Never has so much been owed by so many to so few."

NIGEL. I know exactly how much you owe me.

CONSTANCE. Pardon?

NIGEL. Two thousand seven hundred and forty-three pounds nine and tenpence.

CONSTANCE. Is money all you think about?

NIGEL. You know damn well it isn't.

CONSTANCE. When I think how my position depends on someone as worthless as you, I . . .

MONICA. P.M.!

NIGEL (*sitting up*) No, go on. What were you going to say?

CONSTANCE. Nothing.

NIGEL (*rising*) Yes, you were. You said your position depended on someone like me.

MONICA. A figure of speech.

DAVID. I think what the Prime Minister means . . .

CONSTANCE. Professor!

NIGEL. Let him speak. Go on, David.

DAVID. Well, she explained to me last night, when you were sulking in the bedroom, that the First Lord was more or less about to depose her from office.

NIGEL. You don't say!

DAVID. But while she has us, so to speak, popular support will remain on her side.

NIGEL. Why didn't you tell me this?

DAVID. Is it important?

NIGEL. Important? Do you know what this means?

DAVID. No.

NIGEL. It means that from now on I'm going to call the tune round here. I've been sitting like a stuffed lemon, letting these hens rule the roost. When they depend absolutely on me.

DAVID. There is *me*.

NIGEL. Theoretically.

DAVID. I resent that.

NIGEL. You haven't my romantic appeal.

LYDIA (*moving to* L *of Constance*) I disagree.

NIGEL. But he hasn't my public image. Astronaut, ladies' man of twenty-five—well, twenty years' experience—glamorous uniform —passable profile . . .

MONICA. Ball and chain.

NIGEL. Ah! But every woman loves an under-dog.

MONICA. As long as you've got that round your ankle, you're ours.

NIGEL. Not quite. (*He produces the gun*)

CONSTANCE. Put that away!

NIGEL. Why should I? I'm the only person in this country who can get away with murder. Come one step nearer, and I'll shoot you and offer myself to the Opposition.

CONSTANCE. Over my dead body. (*She moves towards Nigel*)

NIGEL. Why not?

CONSTANCE. This is treason.

NIGEL. Now, do I talk turkey with Helen Marchbanks, or chicken with you?

CONSTANCE. Well, Monica?

MONICA. Just for once, P.M., can't you make up your mind?

CONSTANCE. Lydia?

LYDIA. Don't ask me. I'm through with politics. I'm going to bury myself in the country and breed frogs.

NIGEL (*to Constance*) Well?

CONSTANCE. What are your terms?

NIGEL. That's more like it. First of all . . .

CONSTANCE. Monica, take notes.

MONICA. I beg your pardon?

CONSTANCE. Takes notes of what the Air Marshal is saying.

MONICA. The whom?

NIGEL. You heard. First of all, a hairdresser. Then a masseuse. Then . . .

MONICA. I resign.

NIGEL. You can't. Control of Labour Act. Section thirty-nine.

MONICA. Why, you . . . ! (*She produces a notebook and pencil*)

NIGEL. Next, a blacksmith. In the meantime, send one of your minions to Soho for two dozen bottles of Bollinger 'forty-nine.

(MONICA *crosses to Nigel, writing*)

MONICA. Anything else?

NIGEL. Not quite. (*He takes a little black book from his pocket*) Take this book. (*He gives the book to Monica*) Telephone all the numbers with two red rings and a blue exclamation mark.

MONICA. What do I say?

NIGEL. Tell them Binkum's back in circulation, and get 'em round here at the double.

MONICA. The double? (*She crosses to the door* L)

NIGEL. On second thoughts, send cars.

DAVID (*rising*) Er—Nigel . . .

NIGEL. David, I'd forgotten all about you. What would you like?

DAVID. Well, actually, I'd rather like to go and live in the country somewhere, to devote myself to—er—further biological experiments. (*He moves up* R)

LYDIA. On frogs?

DAVID. Not only frogs.

LYDIA. We could join forces. (*She moves to David*)

DAVID. And do them together?

LYDIA. Why not?

DAVID. What an absolutely splendid idea.
NIGEL. Monica, go and find me a bottle of Scotch.
MONICA. Where from?
NIGEL. That's your problem. (*He crosses to the door* L) And if you don't solve it, I may send *you* to the Outer Hebrides. (*He opens the door*)

(MONICA *exits* L)

Connie, you've been letting her get out of hand.
CONSTANCE (*moving to the sofa and sitting*) I'm letting you get out of hand.
NIGEL. I haven't begun yet. When I really get going I'll make Solomon look like a trappist monk with rheumatism.
CONSTANCE. Take care. Pride comes before a fall.
NIGEL. Not in this case. I tell you, P.M., nothing can stop me now.

(MONICA *enters* L, *agitated and breathless*)

MONICA. They're coming.
NIGEL. That was quick.
MONICA. Not your harem.
NIGEL. Who, then?
MONICA. A mob.
CONSTANCE (*rising*) A mob?
MONICA. Thirty yards from the front gates.
CONSTANCE. But this is England.
MONICA. Listen!

(*They listen. Sounds of a crowd are heard, over the unmistakable tones of a brass band playing "Anchors Away"*)

NIGEL. Good God.
MONICA. It's a band.
CONSTANCE. It's impossible. I must have a look at this. (*She moves to the window*)
MONICA. Don't show yourself. They may be dangerous.

(CONSTANCE *stops*)

DAVID (*moving to the door* R) Take to the cellars.
CONSTANCE. There aren't any.

(LYDIA *follows David*)

DAVID. The attics, then.
NIGEL. Let's see what they want, first.
DAVID. That's obvious.
NIGEL. David . . .
DAVID. They're after us. We'll be—molested.
NIGEL. To the strains of *Anchors Away?*
MONICA. I admit the brass band seems reassuring.
CONSTANCE. It indicates their intention is honourable.

NIGEL. Exactly. If it wasn't they'ld have brought a dozen gipsy fiddlers.

MONICA. I think I'd better take another peek.

(MONICA *exits* L)

LYDIA. I suppose it could be the mob from the Tower.

DAVID. With a band to allay our suspicions. That's it. Right now they're probably surrounding the place. (*He moves to the window*)

(LYDIA *follows David*)

CONSTANCE. Rubbish!

DAVID. Climbing in through windows. Any moment now they'll come bursting through that door. (*He indicates the door* R)

(*The door* R *bursts open.* DAVID *squeals with terror. The* MAJOR *enters* R)

MAJOR. Where's Nige?

(NIGEL *crosses to the Major*)

CONSTANCE. Colonel! What are you doing here?

MAJOR. Having a spree. Da-de-dah, de-dah, bom-bomp!

CONSTANCE. She's drunk.

MAJOR. Nige?

NIGEL. Coming.

MAJOR. I feel queer. What happened?

NIGEL. Read this. (*He thrusts "Fanny Hill" into the Major's hands*) It explains everything.

(NIGEL *pushes the* MAJOR *off* R *and closes the door*)

CONSTANCE. Drunk on duty. I'll have her stripped for this.

NIGEL. Not here.

(MONICA *enters* L)

MONICA. It's the First Lord.

CONSTANCE. Marchbanks!

MONICA. With six coaches and the massed bands of the Townswomen's Guild.

CONSTANCE. The impudence of it.

LYDIA (*crossing to* L) What does she want?

(DAVID *follows* LYDIA)

MONICA. We'll soon know.

CONSTANCE. Probably crawling for her job back.

(DORA *enters* L *and stands to one side*)

DORA (*announcing*) The Chief Wren.

(HELEN *sweeps in* L. DORA *remains by the door* L)

HELEN. What-ho, Connie! These your men?

CONSTANCE. They are. And the operative word is mine.
HELEN. I suppose they are men. Don't look much to me.
CONSTANCE. One can't be choosey these days.
HELEN. Well, as far as I'm concerned you're welcome to them.
NIGEL. Monica, show this Ancient Mariner out, will you?
HELEN. Not till I've had my say. Took your tip about going through the Admiralty files. Found the missing sub. Due in at Tilbury this afternoon.
CONSTANCE. Don't understand.
HELEN. Just met it in.
CONSTANCE. Yourself?
HELEN. Least I could do. You'd expect a welcome if you'd spent the last two years under the North Pole.
CONSTANCE. Did you say two years?
HELEN. Right.
CONSTANCE. Then that means . . .
LYDIA. Men! (*She leads David up* L)
DORA. More men?
HELEN. Of course. That's what I came to tell you.
CONSTANCE. Monica, my smelling salts. (*She staggers to the sofa*)
MONICA (*ignoring Constance*) Where are they?
CONSTANCE. In the bureau.
MONICA. The men.
HELEN. Outside. Six coach-loads.
CONSTANCE. Oh, no! (*She sits on the sofa*)
HELEN. And all Admiralty property.
CONSTANCE. I think I'm going to faint.

(CONSTANCE *puts her hand to her head but the others pay no attention to her*)

MONICA. How many?
HELEN. One hundred and eighty.
DORA. Cor! Let me out.

(DORA *rushes out* L)

CONSTANCE (*rising*) I said I think I'm going to faint.
MONICA. Well, get on with it.

(CONSTANCE *collapses on to the sofa*)

HELEN. Makes your contribution look a bit sick, what?
DAVID. But this is splendid!
NIGEL. It's the end!
CONSTANCE. It's the end all right.
HELEN. I'll be forming my Cabinet next week. With *new* faces. Sorry, Connie, all I can offer you is a peerage. (*She turns to go*)
MONICA (*to Helen*) Prime Minister! Prime Minister!

(HELEN *realizes that she is being addressed, and turns*)

HELEN. Me?

MONICA. Who else? You have your inaugural speech prepared?
HELEN. Speech?
MONICA. It could start, "In this grave hour of want, I am proud but humble to be chosen as the instrument of destiny in bringing new hope into the future of us all."
HELEN. Yes. Yes. Sounds promising.
MONICA. I'll have the first draft ready by the time we reach Town.
HELEN. Fine, fine. I think we'll get on—Monica.
MONICA. I'm sure we shall, P.M.

(HELEN *and* MONICA *exit* L)

CONSTANCE. *Et tu, Brute?*
LYDIA. Never mind, dear. You'll be quite happy in the Lords.
NIGEL. Right now she'd look more at home in the Ladies.
CONSTANCE. Torpedoed by a blasted atomic submarine. Lydia, do you suppose there might be still more men lying around?
LYDIA. In orbit, perhaps.
CONSTANCE. That's it! Space.
NIGEL. We haven't any men in space.
CONSTANCE. But the Yanks might. (*She rises*) I'm off to do a spot of lease-lend.
LYDIA. But . . .
CONSTANCE. No buts. We might even get an option on a Ranger. I'll give you ten minutes to pack. I'm not finished with Marchbanks by a long chalk.

(CONSTANCE *exits* L. LYDIA *crosses to the door* L)

DAVID. Lydia!
LYDIA (*stopping and turning*) Yes?
DAVID. You're not going with her?
LYDIA. I've no choice.
DAVID. But the frogs. (*He moves to Lydia*) Our frogs. Don't they mean more to you than stupid political manœuvres?
LYDIA (*melting*) Of course they do. (*She gives David a self-conscious peck*)
DAVID. What are we waiting for? Let's get as far away from this place as possible.

(DAVID *and* LYDIA *move to the french windows*)

NIGEL. Hey! What about me?
DAVID. Are you interested in frogs?
NIGEL. I'm interested in escape.
LYDIA. Then run for it. Like us.
NIGEL (*indicating the ball and chain*) With this?
LYDIA. We'll post you a hacksaw.

(LYDIA *and* DAVID *exit by the french windows*)

NIGEL. David! (*He hobbles to the window and watches them go. He contemplates his ball and chain and fingers his gun. He puts the ball on the floor, aims the gun at it, puts his forefinger in his left ear, closes his eyes and is about to fire)*

(EVE *enters* L. *She gives a little scream and the gun goes off)*

Eve! I nearly shot my foot off.

EVE. I thought that's what you were trying to do.

NIGEL. I'm not that desperate.

EVE. I'm glad.

NIGEL. Why haven't you joined the Navy?

EVE. Well—I get awfully seasick.

NIGEL. But not airsick?

EVE. No, never.

NIGEL. Darling! (*He embraces Eve and is about to kiss her*)

(HELEN *and* MONICA *appear outside the french windows*)

MONICA. Here he is!

HELEN. Good show!

NIGEL. What do you want?

HELEN. You. (*To Monica*) Get him.

(HELEN *and* MONICA *come into the room*)

NIGEL. Why? You've got half the fleet outside.

HELEN. They're no good.

(CONSTANCE *enters* L)

They're in quarantine, the whole blasted lot of 'em.

NIGEL. What with?

HELEN. Mumps.

NIGEL. Mumps?

HELEN. Didn't tell Connie, of course.

CONSTANCE. But she knows now, you pirate.

HELEN. Quick!

CONSTANCE. Don't touch him. He's mine.

HELEN. He was.

(HELEN, MONICA *and* CONSTANCE *manœuvre* NIGEL *against the sofa*)

EVE. If he's anyone's, he's mine. (*She throws her arms around Nigel*)

(NIGEL *ducks and reaches the door* R.
*The* MAJOR *enters* R)

MAJOR. Nige!

(NIGEL *evades the Major and backs to the french windows.*
DORA *enters* L)

DORA. Lay off him, you lot.

NIGEL *dodges and backs up the bookcase steps, lifting his ball and chain to use as a weapon. He starts to swing it at the six* WOMEN *advancing simultaneously. They close in round the steps and catch hold of his ankles. In resignation, he gives up the fight and slides down the steps into their midst, as—*

*the* CURTAIN *falls*

Blackout

# NOTE TO PRODUCERS

The comedy of this play depends on the ability of the actors to convince their audience that they sincerely believe in the improbable situations in which they find themselves. Each part should therefore be played "straight" and any tendency to overact or burlesque should be resisted.

NIGEL: A gay extrovert who, having always fancied himself as a lady-killer, reacts eagerly to his unique opportunities. In contrast with his boisterous enjoyment of them is his intense indignation when his desires are continually frustrated.

DAVID: A shy introvert, who is appalled at the prospect of being a potential "super-mate", and reacts with alarm and embarrassment in all his contacts with women who regard him as such.

CONSTANCE: Although she appears pompous and haughty with limited intelligence, she is basically shrewd and of strong personality. Her rivalry with Helen is almost an obsession, and her triumph after she has outwitted Helen in Act II must be strongly contrasted with her abjectness when the tables are turned in Act III.

MONICA: A cold, calculating and intelligent woman. She lacks Constance's dominating force and is content to be the "power behind the throne", manœuvring Constance easily and skilfully. She has no conscience and changes her allegiance abruptly when it is in her own interest to do so.

LYDIA: An essentially sympathetic character. Although a dedicated scientist with the appearance of a blue-stocking, she is very much a woman at heart. Her affection for David is not so much the result of frustration as through meeting someone of similar intellect for the first time and her scene with him in Act II should be played with sincerity and pathos.

DORA: Transparently she has only one interest—men. Her natural cockney impudence and contempt for her superiors were aggravated as a result of the catastrophe and, after the discovery of the men, by her suspicion that the politicians are cheating her out of her fair share.

The MAJOR: A heavy, unattractive, female equivalent of a drill sergeant. She takes a sadistic relish in making life uncomfortable for the two astronauts. In Act III she becomes, after her injection, maudling and frighteningly arch.

HELEN: A commanding and forceful "Queen Wren". She is used to getting her own way and is so self-centred that she puts political advancement before the continuance of the race.

EVE: A sex-symbol, young, beautiful, easy-going and vacuous.

# FURNITURE AND PROPERTY LIST

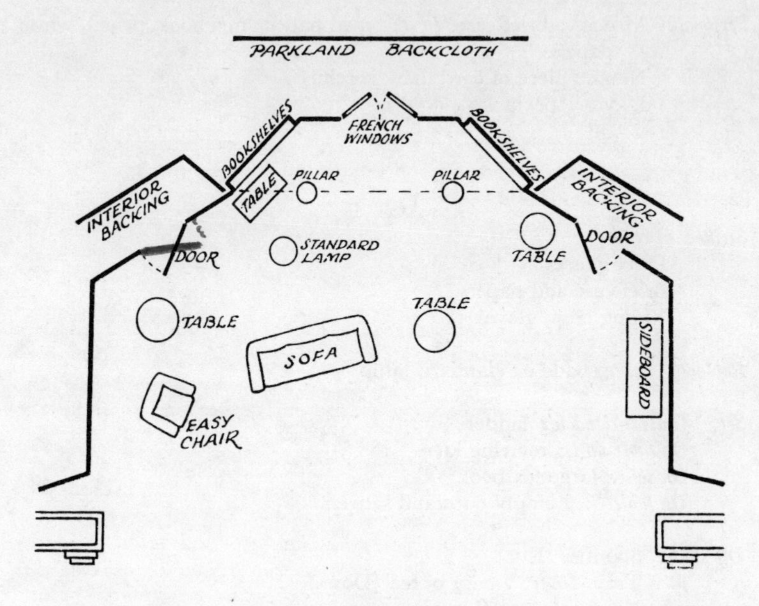


## ACT I

*On stage:* Easy chair (R) *On it:* cushion
*Against wall* R: golf bag with clubs
*On wall* R: picture
Table (R) *On it:* table-lamp
Bell-push (above door R)
Light switch (above door R)
Table (up R) *On it:* record-player, records
Built-in bookshelves (up R and up L) *In them:* books
Table (C) *On it:* sheaf of typed papers
Table (up L) *On it:* Chinese vase
*On wall* L: mirror
Sideboard (L) *On it:* tray, bottles of gin, sherry, tonic, lemon juice; glass, corkscrew, bottle opener
Standard lamp
Window curtains
Carpet on floor
*In door* R: door key

*Off stage:* Riding crop, gloves (CONSTANCE)
Trolley with intravenous feeding device and box with padlock.
*In box:* hypodermic, bottle of fluid, cotton wool, etc. (MAJOR)
Gun (MAJOR)
Boatswain's whistle (DORA)

*Personal:* MONICA: brief-case. *In it:* typed papers, notebook, pencil, white paper
NIGEL: piece of card, handkerchief
DAVID: spectacles

## ACT II

*Strike:* Trolley
Dirty glasses
Brief-case and papers
Riding crop, gloves

*Replace:* Lampshade on standard lamp

*Set:* *Outside window:* ladder
*On table up* L: reviving kit
*On sofa:* large textbook
*On table* C: 2 empty cups and saucers

*Off stage:* Spanner (EVE)
Tray. *On it:* 2 cups of tea (DORA)
Notebook, pen (LYDIA)
Apple (EVE)
Stop-watch (LYDIA)
Tray. *On it:* 2 cups of tea (DORA)
Bottle of scent (DORA)
Greatcoat (EVE)
Tartan rug (DORA)

*Personal:* DAVID: spectacles
LYDIA: spectacles

## ACT III

*Strike:* Cups and saucers
Drinks and bottles
Rug
Bottle of scent

*Set:* *On sofa:* book
Trolley (up L) *On it:* remains of breakfast
*Under table-lamp:* flex for cutting

*On table* C: ashtray, matches
Bookcase steps (up L)

*Reset:* Sofa RC

*Off stage:* Hammer (MAJOR)
Ball and chain (NIGEL)
Cup of tea (DORA)

*Personal:* NIGEL: cigarettes, lighter, small black book
MONICA: notebook and pencil

# LIGHTING PLOT

Property fittings required: table-lamp, standard lamp

Interior. A reception-room. The same scene throughout

THE MAIN ACTING AREAS are the whole stage

THE APPARENT SOURCES OF LIGHT are, in daytime, french windows back C; and at night, a table-lamp R and a standard lamp up R

ACT I. A spring morning

*To open:* Effect of bright sunshine
Fittings off

*No cues*

ACT II. Early evening

*To open:* Effect of sunset
Fittings on

*Cue* 1 After rise of CURTAIN (Page 23)
*Commence slow cross fade from sunset to dusk*

ACT III. Morning

*To open:* Effect of bright sunshine
Fittings off

*No cues*

# EFFECTS PLOT

## ACT I

*Cue* 1 At rise of CURTAIN (Page 1)
*Sound of bird song*

*Cue* 2 CONSTANCE: "And loose." (Page 9)
*Sound of a car arriving and stopping*

*Cue* 3 NIGEL: "Now, be reasonable." (Page 16)
*Sound of dogs barking*

## ACT II

*Cue* 4 At rise of CURTAIN (Page 23)
*Sound of hammering off up* C
*Gramphone music—a Highland reel*

*Cue* 5 NIGEL switches off gramophone (Page 23)
*Stop music*

*Cue* 6 DAVID: "Thank you." (Page 23)
*Hammering ceases*

*Cue* 7 EVE: "How did you guess?" (Page 39)
3 *knocks on door* R

*Cue* 8 NIGEL and Eve kiss (Page 40)
3 *knocks on door* R

*Cue* 9 DAVID: "I can't remember." (Page 42)
3 *knocks on door* R

*Cue* 10 NIGEL switches on record-player (Page 45)
*Music of a Highland Reel*

*Cue* 11 NIGEL opens window (Page 45)
*Alarm rings*

## ACT III

*Cue* 12 At rise of CURTAIN (Page 46)
*Sound of hammering off up* C

*Cue* 13 The MAJOR switches on record-player (Page 52)
*Music of Saint Bernard's Waltz*

*Cue* 14 NIGEL switches off record-player (Page 52)
*Stop music*
2 *loud thuds off* R

*Cue* 15 MONICA: "Listen." (Page 56)
*Sounds of a crowd and a brass band playing* "*Anchors Away.*"

Any character costumes or wigs needed in the performance of this play can be hired from Charles H Fox Ltd, 25 Shelton Street, London WC2H 9HX.

MADE AND PRINTED IN GREAT BRITAIN BY
WHITSTABLE LITHO LTD., WHITSTABLE, KENT